THE NON-PROPHET'S GUIDE™ TO SPIRITUAL WARFARE

TODD HAMPSON

HARVEST HOUSE PUBLISHERS
EUGENE, OREGON

Cover design by Bryce Williamson

Cover illustration by Todd Hampson

Interior design by Chad Dougherty

Published in association with William K. Jensen Literary Agency, 119 Bampton Court, Eugene, Oregon 97404.

Non-Prophet's Guide is a trademark of The Hawkins Children's LLC. Harvest House Publishers, Inc. is the exclusive licensee of the trademark Non-Prophet's Guide.

For bulk, special sales, or ministry purchases, please call 1-800-547-8979. Email: Customerservice@hhpbooks.com

Dedicated to Pastor Keith Koch and Jeff Girdler—
my first pastor and small group leader. I was blessed to have both of you
as spiritual mentors at a critical time in my walk with the Lord.
Along with your wives, Linda and Barb, you have influenced my life,
marriage, children, and ministry more than you know.
Thank you for your steadfast examples and your
faithful dedication to the Lord.

CONTENTS

SECTION 4: Entering the Battle

INTRODUCTION

Are You Prepared?

The thief comes only to steal and kill and destroy;
I have come that they may have life,
and have it to the full.

JOHN 10:10

The Roman soldier stood there exhausted. Four hours of organized formation battle tactics followed by some intense hand-to-hand combat in the dusty summer sun had tested his training and equipment to the limit. With a pause in the action he could assess his wounds and equipment. He knew he was wounded, but the pain from the cut on his lower leg hadn't fully set in. The bleeding had stopped, but the stinging sensation from the gash began to grow as his adrenaline subsided. It's nothing he hadn't felt during his training and in previous battles. The lone wound—a testament to the effectiveness of his armor— would heal fully within a few weeks.

With wound assessment complete, he turned his attention to his equipment. There were a few holes in his shield from the arrows. He would have to repair

5

those right away. Aside from that, he noticed a few fresh dents in his helmet, a scuff on his breastplate, a damaged section of his sword blade that would need sharpening, a few new marks on the protective leather straps that hung from his thick belt, and some bloodstains on his sandal straps resulting from the wound on his leg. Other than that, his equipment would just need a fresh polish before the victory parade when he returned home. Thoughts of that briefly flood his emotions. But his mental toughness kicked in as he reminded himself that there were still more battles to fight before that victorious event became a reality. Now to find a fresh water supply and some shade to rest in and repair his equipment before the next battle…

Think for a moment about your most vivid competitive or physically demanding experience. Perhaps it was a cross-country running event, football game, basketball game, band competition, academic bowl, swim meet, or snowboarding competition. These and a thousand other possibilities come to mind, but insert your experience into the blank space. Now, think about the equipment or uniform required for that activity and how you felt as you warmed up for the event. Each piece had a purpose.

Maybe it was lacing up your cleats, sliding shin guards into your socks, strapping on a bass drum, or warming up your vocals. Whatever the competition or activity, there was a psychological process of getting into the zone—preparing yourself mentally, and might I say spiritually, to step into the fray. For me it was boxing. There's something about the process of putting on your handwraps, gloving up, sliding on your headgear, slapping some grease on your nose, and putting in your mouthpiece that mentally prepares you for the moment when you step between the ropes.

This is analogous to the picture Paul paints for us in Ephesians chapter 6, where he provides instructions for the believer about how to put on spiritual armor. Whether you realize it or not, you are in the middle of a cosmic spiritual war at this very moment and you need spiritual protection. In Ephesians 6:12, the word Paul uses to describe our spiritual struggle is the Greek word *palē*, which refers to close hand-to-hand combat. When we fight spiritual battles, they are close, intense, dangerous—in our face.

We have a very real enemy who comes at us with all the trickery of the fallen world, fallen humanity, and evil forces in the unseen realm. If that weren't enough, our own fallenness is leveraged against us. Our sin nature is real. It is in our DNA from conception. It's the enemy within. Without God's help we are toast. But Paul gives us some clear marching orders and practical insights about successfully contending "against the authorities, against the powers of this dark world and against the spiritual forces of evil in the heavenly realms," as the rest of verse 12 informs us.

For us as believers, the enemy has no ultimate power against us, yet he still does his level best to "steal and kill and destroy," as John 10:10 reveals. So when did this fight start? Why did it start? Who are the players? And why are we caught in the middle?

There exists much misinformation about spiritual warfare. Pop culture paints angels as fat harp-playing babies or winged blond-haired men and women. On the flip side, fallen angels are portrayed in media a thousand different ways—as long as each film or show can scare the audience worse than the previous one.

Because of these and other reasons, the topic of spiritual warfare is confusing, elusive, and scary to many people. Where can we find truth? The good news is that a careful study of Scripture reveals much more information about these matters than one might realize.

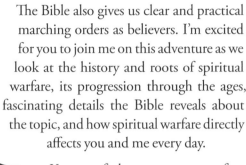

The Bible also gives us clear and practical marching orders as believers. I'm excited for you to join me on this adventure as we look at the history and roots of spiritual warfare, its progression through the ages, fascinating details the Bible reveals about the topic, and how spiritual warfare directly affects you and me every day.

You may feel weary, worn out, fearful, or confused as you view the world around us and as you fight your personal battles each day. Read on and you'll discover the secrets to fighting successfully and finishing strong. God equips us to stand firm until the final bell has rung. And when the battle is over, it will all be worth it as we hear the words, "Well done, good and faithful servant! You have been faithful with a few things; I will put you in charge of many things. Come and share your master's happiness!" (Matthew 25:23).

But between that moment and where you stand right now lie many battles to be fought. If you and I apply what God's Word shares, we can emerge as overcoming victors with the help of the Lord. Let the training begin!

The Non-Prophet

THE NON-PROPHET

He's a Renaissance man. The ultimate throwback. The Non-Prophet is a 501(c)(3) that seems to have been born in 501 BC. He prefers the clothing, speech, food, facial grooming (or lack thereof), and customs of an archetypical Old Testament prophet living in twenty-first century America. He misunderstands Bible prophecy and gives well-meaning but poor advice. The Non-Prophet is also not very wise with money, so he's a Non-Prophet on two levels. He's the epitome of the idiom "a day late and a dollar short."

Stuart Dent (Student)

Stuart Dent, aka "Stu" (to his family) or "Dent" to most of his friends. Stu Dent is a veteran and is now enrolled in seminary. A mentor led him to the Lord during his time of service and now God has called him to prepare for full-time ministry. Stu just registered for classes on angelology and spiritual warfare so he's doing a bit of early study. He assumes by the Non-Prophet's garb that his prophetic-looking friend is a wise sage who can help him get up to speed on the topics at hand. Fortunately for Stu, his own discernment and intelligence help him learn about the topic accurately despite the Non-Prophet's faulty teaching.

STUART "STU" DENT

Dee Sipel (Disciple)

DEE SIPEL

Dee is a friend of Dent's from the Bible college. They met the previous semester and realized they both have a passion for theology and ministry. Dee notices small details and loves wrestling with concepts until she can see how it all fits together. This aspect of her personality and gifting makes sense because Dee works as a crime-scene investigator. She attends Bible college part time and plans to get a degree in Christian apologetics.

SECTION 1:

UNDERSTANDING THE BATTLE

CHAPTER 1

Pre-Genesis History

Your throne was established long ago;
you are from all eternity.

PSALM 93:2

Lawrence Peter Berra was born in St. Louis, Missouri on May 12, 1925. He died on September 22, 2015 after playing 19 seasons (all but the last four with the New York Yankees) of Major League Baseball and spending many more years as a manager and coach.

"Yogi" Berra, as he was nicknamed, was famous for many things related to baseball, not the least of which were his world-famous statements that came to be known as *Yogi-Berraisms*. His comical and perfectly timed paradoxical quips frequently appeared as sports news headlines.

Here are five of my personal favorites:

"It ain't over till it's over."

"It's like déjà vu all over again."

"A nickel ain't worth a dime anymore."

"We made too many wrong mistakes."

"The future ain't what it used to be."[1]

YOGI BERRA

At this point you may be wondering what Yogi Berra quotes have to do with spiritual warfare. Well, I bring these up because it seems a good place to start this study of spiritual warfare sounds a bit like a Yogi-Berraism. In order to properly understand the very real environment of spiritual warfare in which you and I live today, a great place for us to begin is…before the beginning.

Before the Beginning—Eternity Past

Before the creation of time, space, and matter, God was. God has always existed. He is the great "I AM" (Exodus 3:14). We can't fully wrap our minds around this fact, but that is a good thing because we are not God. Even from a logical and philosophical standpoint, humans intuitively understand God's eternal nature and power must exist. Logically, there has to have been a first cause of everything that exists in our space-time continuum. This is known as the *cosmological argument*.

Romans 1:20—Since the creation of the world God's invisible qualities—his eternal power and divine nature—have been clearly seen, being understood from what has been made, so that people are without excuse.

In my book *The Non-Prophet's Guide™ to the End Times*, I wrote at length about the nature of God and demonstrated how he is outside of time. In chapter 2 of that book I wrote, "We're 'stuck' in time, which we experience linearly, but God by his very nature is outside of time. He created it; therefore, he transcends it. To God, time is more like an object than a chronological experience."[2]

To God, space, matter, and time (and everything within them) are things he beholds at one glance—similar to how a person can view all the activity in a handheld ant farm with clear plastic panels. God sees everything simultaneously. Nothing is hidden from his view and nothing happens outside of his sovereign design. Not a single atom, planck length (smallest unit of space), or planck time (smallest unit of time) is out of his control. He is completely transcendent and sovereign.

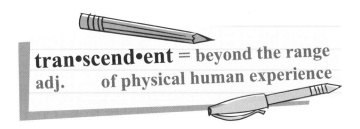

tran•scend•ent = beyond the range
adj.   of physical human experience

With that understanding it is also important to note here that the Trinity—the three persons that comprise God as revealed in Scripture via the Father, Son, and Holy Spirit—existed in perfect fellowship from eternity past. The idea of a three-in-one monotheistic and self-existent God is a great mystery to us—as is the nature of a timeless eternity past. Yet logic demands that something or someone has existed from eternity past. If anything exists, then something or someone has always had to exist. Something can't come from nothing.

Once again, that may sound a bit like a Yogi Berra quote. But, even atheists—who believe the big bang exploded a subatomic "singularity" into 100 billion galaxies stretching 93 billion light-years in diameter—can't answer the philosophical question regarding where that "singularity" came from or what initially triggered it. Their cosmology—when pushed—does not answer the fundamental questions about the existence of space, time, and matter, or the fixed rules that govern them.

One thing we learn from the self-existent triune nature of God is that before any beings existed, he was not lonely or lacking relationship. He is eternally complete in himself. In eternity past, he was perfectly content, living in perfect unity and fellowship with himself—in need of nothing. Yet something about his nature and perfection demanded that at some point the self-existent Creator would create other moral autonomous beings—first the angels, then we humans.

Why Did God Allow Evil to Exist?

Sticking with our Yogi Berra theme, I'd like to pose the question this way: Why did God make any bad good stuff? In other words, why would he even allow for the possibility of evil? God could have done one of four things. He had the choice to:

1. create nothing;
2. create a universe with no possibility of good or evil;
3. create beings with no free will (eliminating the ability to choose good or evil), or;
4. create beings with the capacity of free will.

The final option is the only choice that allows for love because love requires having the freedom to choose. As 1 John 4:8 tells us, God is love. Love can only be expressed if there is a real choice to exhibit it. Love can only be expressed through real sacrifice—logically necessary for putting the needs of others above our own. The essence of God's nature is love. This, I believe, is the central reason why God created the universe, and it is why he created moral agents with freewill—first the angels, then humans.

That gives us the answer to the question that can be answered by the four possibilities listed above: If God never created other beings, love could not be expressed. If God created the universe with no possibility of good and evil, love could not be expressed. If God created cookie-cutter robots that were preprogrammed to obey, love could not be expressed. But if God created moral beings with the freedom to choose, God's nature could be demonstrated through their free-choice actions and ultimately through the sacrificial love *he* would personally have to demonstrate.

> John 3:16—God so loved the world that he gave his one and only Son, that whoever believes in him shall not perish but have eternal life.

When Were Angels Created?

Now that we've answered the *why* question, let's ask the *when* question. To find the answer, we must look to God's revealed Word. We understand from Job 38:7 (where angels shouted for joy as they observed creation) that God produced the angels before he created the world. Whether this was hours before or millennia before, we do not know. We have some evidence that this may have occurred relatively close to the creation of mankind. Hebrews 1:14 asks the rhetorical question, "Are not all angels ministering spirits sent to serve those who will inherit salvation?" If this is their main function, perhaps it makes sense that they would have been created close to the time frame when mankind was created, although we can't be dogmatic about this. Supporting this idea further is the fact that, in Scripture, *angel* means "messenger." Who would they be messengers or ministering spirits to if not humans?

Creation: Foundations Attacked

Although this chapter concerns pre-Genesis history, for us to understand evil and spiritual warfare, it's necessary for us to look at the Bible's account of origins to show (in the next chapter) how and why Satan rebelled—and how Adam and Eve's fall into sin had cosmic repercussions that reverberated through all of creation and history. In addition, I also want to highlight the Genesis record of origins because no other aspect of Scripture has been more attacked and maligned the past 150 years than the biblical creation account.

The theory of evolution is so thoroughly engrained in educational systems, governments, entertainment, and even some religions that few slow down long enough to consider its claims in the light of plain logic and continually emerging scientific facts. It is a worldview that shifts worship away from the Creator to the things that were created—which is what Romans chapter 1 told us would happen. For various reasons we'll discuss in this book, this is—without question in my mind—a carefully planned minefield laid by the enemy to weaken the foundations of the gospel and the trust people have in God's Word. Satan has done all this for some very specific end-time purposes.

Romans 1:21-23—Although they knew God, they neither glorified him as God nor gave thanks to him, but their thinking became futile and their foolish hearts were darkened. Although they claimed to be wise, they became fools and exchanged the glory of the immortal God for images made to look like a mortal human being and birds and animals and reptiles.

The idea of a literal six-day creation week, or even the idea that everything we observe must have had an intelligent designer, is ridiculed by people who hold to a secular (without God) worldview. Over the past 20 years, the study of molecular biology and new discoveries about DNA have greatly weakened the theory of evolution—to the point where many evolutionists openly admit the theory has problems. Alternative ideas have been proposed, such as the idea that humans were "seeded" here from an alien race. But this type of deceptive speculation still does not answer the question of origins.

I find it very interesting that the belief in the Genesis account of creation, a global flood during the time of Noah, and the future return of the Lord are all topics that have become the focus of spiritual warfare. In 2 Peter 3, we learn that as the church age draws to a close, we should expect to see a widespread mocking of three things in particular: the creation account, the global flood, and the return of the Lord. We should also observe a growing belief in uniformitarianism—the idea that conditions have not changed much at all through the ages but have continued onward a uniform fashion. Read 2 Peter 3:3-6 carefully and see if you can spot these prophetic indicators.

> Above all, you must understand that in the last days *scoffers will come,* scoffing and following their own evil desires. They will say, "*Where is this 'coming' he promised?* Ever since our ancestors died, *everything goes on as it has since the beginning* [uniformitarianism] of creation." But they *deliberately forget that long ago by God's word the heavens came into being and the earth was formed* [creation] out of water and by water. *By these waters also the world of that time was deluged* [Noah's flood] and destroyed (emphasis added).

If the enemy can ruin these foundational truths—at least in the minds of the people whom he wants to deceive—then everything else crumbles. It is no wonder that the biblical account of creation has been so attacked and vilified as the end of the church age plays out.

Peeking Behind the Curtain

Though God has lived in perfect peace and unity from eternity, his very nature required him to create everything *ex nihilo* (out of nothing), including moral beings with the ability to choose to follow God or rebel against him. Though we may struggle now with the reality of evil and pain, one day all will be made right and all will make perfect sense. We intuitively understand there is much we still don't understand; it is still hidden behind the curtain, so to speak. In the next few chapters we'll peek behind the curtain to see exactly how evil began, how things function in the unseen realm, and how we got caught up in the great cosmic war in which we find ourselves embroiled (whether we realize it or not).

Now that we have taken a Yogi Berra-inspired trip from before the beginning up to the time of creation, we need to wrestle with the details related to the origins of spiritual warfare. As we move from the mind-bending concepts of the nature of God and eternity past to the nature of angels and the original cosmic coup attempt (which are presented in the next chapter), we will be dealing with some complex concepts about events that took place in the unseen realm. Buckle up, then, for an exciting ride as we take a look at the beginning of an age-old cosmic war.

CHAPTER 2

Angels and Fallen Angels Explained

How you are fallen from heaven,
O Lucifer, son of the morning!
How you are cut down to the ground,
you who weakened the nations!

ISAIAH 14:12 (NKJV)

If you have ever worked with either page-layout or word-processing software packages, you may be familiar with guides and reveal codes. Design software such as Adobe InDesign and Adobe Illustrator have various guides that you can turn on or off. These guides can show you page edges, margins, alignments, dimensions, and several other normally hidden things. Word-processing software such as Microsoft Word has a feature called *reveal codes* that allows for the display all kinds of hidden things like spaces, tabs, indents, etc. Every unseen code can be seen when the reveal codes feature is enabled.

Whether we realize it or not, there is an unseen realm that is operating right alongside of ours. Because of our fallen nature we are unable to see it, but Scripture reveals to us many details about this unseen realm. In a few of those accounts the reveal codes feature was turned on and the veil was pulled back so that we could see this very real spiritual dimension.

This hidden code running in the background influences much more in our world than most people realize. Theologians have taught this for millennia. Scientists are beginning to catch up. The deeper that physicists look into subatomic particles, and the further out that astrophysicists peer into the vast regions and features of space, the more they are faced with mysteries that intersect with the unseen realm.

If you have taken notice of the phenomenal success of comic-book-inspired movies over the past 10 to 20 years, you've probably bumped into terms like *multiverse*, *string theory*, *tesseracts*, *quantum physics*, *black holes*, and *dark matter*. The backstory to many a comic-book-inspired movie usually integrates elements of these and other brain-cramping concepts.

The past 70 years or so have introduced us to a new era of understanding about the nature of our space-time continuum. The speed of light is not constant as once thought. Light bends. Time slows down or speeds up depending on location and gravity. Quarks disappear and simultaneously reappear in another location. We can't time travel or move in and out of dimensions at will, but modern theoretical mathematics and quantum physics have demonstrated that there is much more than meets the eye to things we once thought to be constants. The fact is, science is catching up to what Scripture has said all along.

"FOR THE SCIENTIST WHO HAS LIVED BY HIS FAITH IN THE POWER OF REASON, THE STORY ENDS LIKE A BAD DREAM. HE HAS SCALED THE MOUNTAINS OF IGNORANCE; HE IS ABOUT TO CONQUER THE HIGHEST PEAK; AS HE PULLS HIMSELF OVER THE FINAL ROCK, HE IS GREETED BY A BAND OF THEOLOGIANS WHO HAVE BEEN SITTING THERE FOR CENTURIES."[1]

—ROBERT JASTROW, *GOD AND THE ASTRONOMERS*

What Scripture teaches from the outset is that our reality doesn't operate independently from the unseen realm. Using our analogy from above, the divine reveal codes are the driving force behind the curtain, and this larger unseen reality intersects with many aspects of our physical world.

Originally heaven and earth were melded in a major way. Eden is pictured in Scripture as a garden where God interacted directly with mankind (Genesis 3:8). The fall of man fractured that original setup. In modern-day mathematic and comic book lingo, the dimensions became fractured, resulting in a parallel dimension that exists alongside of ours. The last two chapters of the book of Revelation speak of the restoration of the world to an Edenic state—putting things back to the way God originally intended.

You may be thinking, *This is some weird stuff*, or *This is amazing!*—or perhaps a little of both. I agree. We are so used to our daily routines and our uniform sensory existence that we easily overlook the much bigger reality that exists just behind the molecular veil. Get ready for some more weird stuff. The next three chapters will offer plenty. I highly encourage you to prayerfully consider what Scripture has to say about everything we'll be discussing. The second half of this book is all practical application (how to apply the full armor of God to our daily lives and struggles), but the first half lays a necessary theological foundation so we understand exactly what we are up against. To our modern sensibilities, it is indeed some weird stuff—but 100 percent real.

God's Cabinet

In America, each president has a cabinet. Not the kind you store dishes in, but the kind you store leadership in. The president's cabinet is made up of the vice president and the heads of each executive department. They are his key advisors, each one focused on a critical aspect of national concern.

CHART OF ADVISORY BOARDS

1. **Non-Profit Board**
2. **Presidential Cabinet**
3. **Military Advisory Board**
4. **Board of Directors**
5. **Elders/Deacons Board**

This kind of advisory council is common for any large organization or form of government. Kings have a court of advisors. Company CEOs have key department heads. By law, nonprofit organizations must have a board of directors. These structures are put in place for accountability, advice, and implementation.

It may surprise you to learn that God has a cabinet—a divine council known as the heavenly court. He doesn't need advice or accountability because he is all-knowing and perfectly righteous and holy. But he values relationship and chose to involve his creatures in the privilege of carrying out his universe-governing will. We discover this council early in Scripture, and we witness its culmination in various accounts of end-time events (depicted in Daniel and Revelation). Consider the following verses:

> The heavens praise your wonders, LORD, your faithfulness too, in the assembly of the holy ones...In the council of the holy ones God is greatly feared; he is more awesome than all who surround him (Psalm 89:5,7).

> When the Most High assigned lands to the nations, when he divided up the human race, he established the boundaries of the peoples according to the number in his heavenly court (Deuteronomy 32:8 NLT).

> One day the angels [literally, "sons of God"] came to present themselves before the LORD, and Satan [literally, "the adversary"] also came with them (Job 1:6).

> Thousands upon thousands attended him; ten thousand times ten thousand stood before him. The court was seated, and the books were opened (Daniel 7:10).

When studying this topic, you may also bump into a couple of other phrases that can be confusing if you don't know the proper context. For example, in the Old Testament passages cited here, the phrases "sons of God" or "holy ones" refer to angels, who are heavenly creations of God. For simplicity, from this point onward, I will (for the most part) use the terms *angels* and *fallen angels* to categorize heavenly beings.

QUICK FACT: DID YOU KNOW...
that the word *angel* simply means "messenger"?

The throne room sits at the center of the divine council, and it is here that God makes his decrees and sends angels to carry them out. Using our cabinet theme—the throne room is like God's Oval Office. In Scripture, we catch a few glimpses of the throne room—most notably in Ezekiel chapter 1, Isaiah chapter 6, and Revelation chapters 4–6 and 15. These passages provide the most detailed descriptions of God's throne room and divine council. I recommend you take the time to do a further study of them.

Though God is spirit and is omnipresent (John 4:24; Acts 17:28), he rules from heaven's throne room—a literal place that is surrounded by members of his council. After Jesus's ascension, we find him—whenever the throne room is mentioned thereafter—sitting at the right hand of God's throne. In Revelation 4 we find—in this future glimpse after the rapture of the church—an additional 24 elders (key church leaders or representatives of the church) present in the divine council.

The Primary Cosmic Rebellion

Satan, or the adversary, was originally called Lucifer. He was a beautiful creature of extreme heavenly privilege. You can read about his original state, rebellion, and fall in Isaiah 14:12-14 and Ezekiel 28:14-18. Lucifer, one of God's highest (if not the highest) angels, was a guardian cherub—a magnificent creature who stood before God's throne. His name means "light bearer." His role as throne guardian led to rebellious pride. Rather than recognizing his extreme privilege, he lusted for more power and was self-deceived into thinking he could usurp God's throne.

Ezekiel 28:14-15—You were anointed as a guardian cherub, for so I ordained you. You were on the holy mount of God; you walked among the fiery stones. You were blameless in your ways from the day you were created till wickedness was found in you.

During his initial rebellion, Satan convinced one-third of the heavenly beings to join him. Following this, these divine beings were eternally locked into their choice of sides, with no chance of redemption. Fallen angels would remain fallen, and holy angels would remain holy—set apart for service to God. By the way, we learn about a similar earthly version of this scenario that will occur during the future seven-year tribulation period. Those who choose to worship the antichrist and take the mark of the beast will be locked into their choice with no chance of redemption (Revelation 14:9-11).

We do not know exactly when Satan's fall occurred, but we learn from Job 38:4-7 that all the angelic beings watched God create the earth and rejoiced. It does not appear that Satan had rebelled prior to this point. We are told in Genesis 1:31–2:1 that after creation, God saw all he had created, and it was "very good." This tells us Satan's fall occurred sometime between creation and the tempting of Adam and Eve.

SATAN'S TITLES

John 12:31	Prince of This World
Ephesians 2:2	Prince of the Power of the Air
Matthew 4:1	The Devil
2 Corinthians 4:4	God of This Age

The Guardian Cherub Rebels

As we look at the fall of Satan and other angelic rebellions, first I'd like to highlight a curious fact. Even after rebelling, fallen angels seem to maintain their rank or position—at least for now. Notice in the book of Job that even after Satan fell, he was allowed to attend the gathering of the divine council:

> One day the angels came to present themselves before the Lord, and Satan also came with them. The Lord said to Satan, "Where have you come from?" Satan answered the Lord, "From roaming throughout the earth, going back and forth on it" (1:6-7).

> On another day the angels came to present themselves before the Lord, and Satan also came with them to present himself before him. And the Lord said to Satan, "Where have you come from?" Satan answered the Lord, "From roaming throughout the earth, going back and forth on it" (Job 2:1-2).

What we find in Scripture is that when it comes to redemption and judgment, God's activity usually happens in phases.

As for judgment, Satan's initial rebellion got him expelled from heaven—but he was still allowed access to God's council (Job 1:6-12; Ezekiel 28:14-16; Zechariah 3:1-2). According to Scripture, Satan is currently known as "the prince of the power of the air" (Ephesians 2:2 NKJV). This seems to imply that he has free rein to move and operate anywhere within the earth's atmosphere (in the seen and unseen realms).

At the midpoint of the future tribulation period, Satan will be cast from all heavenly realms and restricted to earth's surface alone (Revelation 12:7-13). Then at the end of the tribulation, he will be bound for 1,000 years in a prison known as "the Abyss" (Revelation 20:1-3). Finally, after the millennial kingdom, Satan will be thrown into the lake of fire, where he will be punished for eternity (Revelation 20:10).

The Nature and Types of Angels

Scripture does not provide all the details we would like to have regarding the various kinds of angels or their rank structure, but there are a number of key details revealed to us. I have covered as many of those details as I could in this single chapter, but entire courses (or doctoral degrees, for that matter) can be taken on the topic of angels and demons.

In his thorough (and highly recommended) work *The Mighty Angels of Revelation*,[2] author Nathan Jones details 72 instances of individual and entire groups of angels and demons. For a snapshot of the various kinds of angels that exist, his book is a tremendous resource. Perhaps there is as much variety in the unseen realm as there is in the seen. Why would we think God would resort to less variety when he created angelic beings than he did when he created animals and mankind?

The net result of this initial rebellion is that the unseen realm is inhabited by fallen and unfallen angels. Scripture indicates there are many different kinds of angels, as well as a ranking hierarchy in place—regardless of whether an angel is fallen or not (Jude 9).

2 CORINTHIANS 12:2

The good guys outnumber the bad guys 2 to 1. The bad guys cannot enter the third heaven (God's dwelling place) but are—apparently—free to move about the first and possibly the second heaven (the earth's atmosphere and what we refer to as space).

The Good Guys

Cherubim and seraphim are depicted as very high-ranking throne guardians—perhaps the highest ranking among the heavenly beings. Ezekiel 28:14 informs us that Satan was a cherub, describing him as "the anointed cherub who covers" (NKJV).

Cherubim and seraphim are multifaceted hybrid creatures (see Ezekiel 1:5-14), usually described in the context of guarding God's throne and holiness. Seraphim have six wings (Isaiah 6:2), and cherubim have four. Seraphim are also referred to in Revelation as "four living creatures" (4:6,8). Cherubim are described in Ezekiel as God's mobile throne drivers (Ezekiel 10). Going back to our Oval Office and cabinet analogies, these creatures are like God's top-tier secret service agents—stationed to guard and protect (and in the case of the cherubim, move) the holy throne of God.

CHERUBIM

SERAPHIM 1

SERAPHIM 2

SERAPHIM 3

SERAPHIM 4

Then there are archangels or chief angels. They are leaders of other lower-ranked angels, and they serve God by carrying out his decrees and purposes. Archangels seem to be lower in rank than cherubim and seraphim (based on Ezekiel 28:14 and Jude 9), but they are still higher-ranking than the rest of the angelic beings.

The term *archangel* is used only twice in Scripture (1 Thessalonians 4:16 and Jude 9). Some fallen archangels evidently influence geographical areas in the unseen realm and fight against God's holy angels (Daniel 10:13).

Daniel 10:13 informs us that Michael the archangel is "one of the chief princes." Michael seems to be the military commander of the Lord's armies (Revelation 12:7) and the protector of the Jewish people (Daniel 12:1).

Gabriel is the only other named archangel in Scripture, and his main function is to announce events related to the Messiah (Daniel 9:21; Luke 1:26-28). Daniel describes Gabriel's appearance (9:21)—and other angels he encountered (10:5,16,18)—as that of "the man" or "a man." In some of Daniel's descriptions, angels are described with supernatural features such as a face of lightning, eyes like blazing fire, and glowing arms and legs (10:5-6). Gabriel, though never described as having wings, was also described by Daniel as having the ability to fly swiftly (9:21).

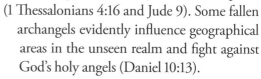

ARCHANGEL MICHAEL

We discover in other portions of Scripture that angels can enter—and interact with—our physical realm. We find them eating meals with humans (Genesis 18:7-8), fighting (2 Kings 19:35), and grabbing humans by the hand (Genesis 19:16). Hebrews 13:2 states that some people have interacted with angels without even realizing they were not human.

ARCHANGEL GABRIEL

> Hebrews 13:2—Do not forget to show hospitality to strangers, for by so doing some people have shown hospitality to angels without knowing it.

The Bible does indicate that believers in Christ (and possibly small children) have guardian angels (Matthew 18:10; Hebrews 1:14). We don't know whether this system of protection is set up as a man-to-man or zone defense, but Hebrews 1:14 reveals this much to us: "Are not all angels ministering spirits sent to serve those who will inherit salvation?" It is humbling to think that just beyond the veil—and possibly in our physical reality—angels are tasked with protecting and ministering to those know Christ as Savior.

The Bad Guys

While holy angels are tasked with serving God and carrying out his redemptive plans for mankind, fallen angels attempt to thwart God's plans and submit to the direction of Satan, the highest-ranking fallen angel. The fallen angels in the unseen realm are also called demons and unclean spirits.

A demon/unclean spirit can influence or even inhabit people who are not born-again believers in Christ. When someone accepts Christ as Savior, they are indwelt (and sealed) by the Holy Spirit (1 Corinthians 6:19-20; Ephesians 1:13-14). A demon cannot occupy the person who is sealed and protected by the presence of the Spirit. Some theologians assert that demons and fallen angels are different types of evil beings. We'll discuss this further in an upcoming chapter.

Based on biblical accounts, demonic activity is characterized by one or more of the following: violence, great strength, self-mutilation, public nudity, shouting, seizures, foaming at the mouth, and more (see Mark 5; 9; Matthew 8; Luke 8; Acts 19).

Demons are given access to humans (even inadvertently) through various occult practices. We should avoid things like Ouija boards, tarot cards, New Age practices, religious yoga, drug use, fascination with demonic or dark themes, seances, astrology, mediums, witchcraft, or any secret or forbidden practices. These things can—intentionally or unintentionally—open the way for demonic possession or oppression to occur.

QUICK FACT: HAVE YOU NOTICED...

that everything in the list above has found its way into the pop culture of our day?

Based on the record of the New Testament, we learn that demons long to inhabit humans so they can interact with the physical realm. We also discover these facts: It is possible for multiple demons to inhabit a single person; demons know who Jesus is and that they will be punished at an appointed future time; demons can inhabit animals; and they recognize the authority of Jesus—whether they encounter him personally or those who are his true followers (See Matthew 8; Mark 5; Luke 8; 9; Acts 19).

Before the flood of Noah's day, a select group of fallen angels was guilty of producing what are believed to be angelic-human hybrids (Genesis 6:1-4; Jude 6-7; 2 Peter 2:4-6). We'll cover this in detail in chapter 4, where we'll tackle this subject in greater depth.

What Gives?

Okay, so there's a cosmic war in the unseen realm. What's it all about? What is the main issue, and when did it start? Why is there a veil between the physical and spiritual realms? Is this how it has always been? How did the universe get into its current state? These are all logical questions stemming from the discussion above. We'll begin our search for answers in the next chapter.

CHAPTER 3

The Crux of the Issue

I will put enmity
between you and the woman,
and between your offspring and hers;
he will crush your head,
and you will strike his heel.

GENESIS 3:15

For some reason, my wife and daughter love watching real-life crime shows. You know, the ones that are narrated by a soothing, soft-spoken voice actor you never see. Though I have never chosen on my own to watch an episode of one of these shows, if my wife or daughter turns on an episode and I watch the first two minutes, I'm hooked and must watch the entire episode in order to learn how the mystery was solved.

These shows usually feature crimes that are nearly impossible to solve without some piece of key evidence or groundbreaking forensic science. This is what makes the shows so compelling. For most of the crimes featured, the scant evidence makes them confusing and seemingly unsolvable—until the moment of breakthrough comes along and helps to unlock the mystery.

There is an often-overlooked bit of biblical mystery that—once understood—causes many other biblical details to suddenly come into clear focus. The first prophecy of a coming Messiah contains a key element that causes the rest of the biblical narrative to make much more sense once it's understood. This single piece of biblical forensic evidence brings much clarity to the nature of spiritual warfare.

For example, confusing commands from God instructing Joshua to wipe out entire people groups in the Promised Land of Canaan suddenly make sense. The perplexing statement in Genesis 6:12 about "all the people on earth" being "corrupted" is better understood. The real reason for the attempts by Pharaoh—and later, Herod—to destroy an entire generation of Jewish boys is understood with newfound clarity.

The significance of these and many other baffling matters are brought into clear focus once we have a clear grasp of the first prophecy in Scripture about the redeemer. Before we highlight that prophecy, however, we must first lay a bit of groundwork to properly set the context. This requires us to understand the nature of the fall and the identity of the serpent.

The Fall

At some point after God created Adam and Eve as his image-bearers, Satan rebelled—yet maintained access to Eden. There he tempted the first man and woman to sin. Scripture seems to indicate that Eden was a place where heaven and earth were melded together—a paradise where the seen and unseen realms functioned as one. Eden is depicted in Scripture as a lush garden (Genesis 2:8; Ezekiel 28:13) as well as a high mountain (Ezekiel 28:16). This mountaintop garden was heaven on earth—a special place where a loving, relational God could live among his creation. We are told that God (most likely the pre-incarnate Jesus) literally walked with Adam and Eve there (Genesis 3:8). Somehow, Satan the deceiver also had access to this perfect paradise. It makes sense (and there are some biblical clues) that Eden was where the divine council met. If you'll recall from the previous chapter, Satan, though fallen, maintained access to that area of heaven.

Scripture informs us that Eden was located somewhere near the Tigris and Euphrates Rivers (Genesis 2:8-14). I say *was* because the Earth's topography was drastically changed due to the flood of Noah's day. It's possible that these two rivers remained as post-flood valleys after the floodwaters receded and maintained their original locations. However, some theologians and Bible-believing scientists deduce that when the post-flood world was repopulated, people named the two most prominent post-flood rivers after the original Tigris and Euphrates, which means we don't know their original locations.

Various church fathers and prominent theologians from the past few centuries have taught that Jerusalem could very well be the original location of Eden—and that this area may also be where the divine council meets in the hidden realm of angelic beings.

I'm not personally dogmatic about either view of where Eden was (modern-day Iraq or Jerusalem), but it is worth the time for each of us to study and prayerfully consider them. In any case, Eden was unlike anything we experience today. Adam and Eve had access to this original paradise where heaven and earth were one—and where God (and other heavenly beings) regularly interacted with them.

In my book *The Non-Prophet's Guide™ to the Book of Revelation*, I highlighted the critical link between the books of Genesis and Revelation. Certain themes introduced in Genesis find their ultimate resolution in Revelation.

This is true for theology and the divinely inspired metanarrative of Scripture. It is also true of the details between God's original design in Genesis and the future restoration of this design in Revelation. For example, the tree of life was located in the middle of the garden of Eden (Genesis 2:9), and we discover this same tree of life currently exists in a place called "the paradise of God" (Revelation 2:7). Finally, we are told that after the tribulation period and the millennial kingdom, God will create a new heaven and new earth with a new Jerusalem, where the tree of life will permanently reside.

The Mysterious Serpent

Though you and I understand the serpent in the garden to be Satan, what may surprise you about the Genesis account is that we are not given any information other than it was a serpent. We reason from the symbolism and the broad context that this serpent was Satan. Our spiritual adversary is also depicted in Scripture as "the great dragon" (Revelation 12:9).

This is where interpreting Scripture with Scripture is so important. We don't learn definitively who the dragon-serpent is until we get to the final chapters of the last book of the Bible. In Revelation 20:2, we are explicitly told that Satan *is* the serpent *and* the dragon spoken of throughout the pages of the Bible.

> Revelation 20:2—He seized the dragon, that ancient serpent, who is the devil, or Satan, and bound him for a thousand years.

Theologians differ on whether or not the serpent was literally Satan, Satan appearing as a serpent, Satan possessing a serpent, or Satan deceiving Adam and Eve into believing it was the serpent speaking. If we dig into the deeper layers of the word meaning, I think we find our answer.

The noun form of the word translated "serpent" in the Genesis account is *nachash* (pronounced naw-khawsh). Important to our discussion is the fact that—when used in adjective form—the root word can also be interpreted "brazen one" or "shiny one." We find some validation of this type of usage in the account of Moses raising a bronze snake on a pole (Numbers 21:9). *Lucifer* (Satan's original name) means "light bringer." This theme is consistent in Scripture. In fact, 2 Corinthians 11:14 clearly informs us that "Satan himself masquerades as an *angel of light*" (emphasis added), and Jesus described the fall of Satan as lightning-like (Luke 10:18).

If the noun and adjective forms of the root word *nachash* weren't theologically interesting enough, consider this fact: The verb form of the word can mean "deceiver." The enemy we know as Satan fits all three forms of the root word—and this sheds a much brighter light on the "serpent" who tempted Adam and Eve.

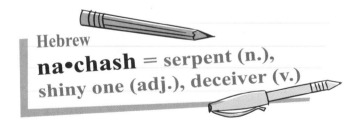

Hebrew
na•chash = serpent (n.), shiny one (adj.), deceiver (v.)

As noted in the previous chapter, cherubim and seraphim are multifaceted hybrid creatures. Could it be that Lucifer the guardian cherub (Ezekiel 28:14) was a similar "living creature" who appeared more dragon- or snake-like in appearance? I believe so. Supporting this idea even further is the fact that the noun *seraph* can also mean "serpent."

I am convinced that Satan— the light-bearing guardian cherub—was not a grotesque, slithering figure who sidled up to Adam and Eve, but a mesmerizingly beautiful heavenly being. Though fallen, he could still at least *appear* as an angel of light. If Eden was heaven on earth and the location of the divine council, Adam and Eve would have been used to seeing cherubim, seraphim, and other heavenly creatures there.

This may explain why Satan's approach did not send them fleeing in terror. His presence didn't initially set off any alarm bells. They trusted him. Satan seemed like someone good and beautiful to them. By the way, isn't that how temptation always works? It looks attractive and fulfilling even though it is selling a destructive lie. This characterized the first temptation—and it established the template for every other temptation to follow. Satan is a master deceiver, a destroyer, and a murderer at heart. These key attributes of our adversary are seen throughout the pages of Scripture.

Once Adam and Eve took the bait, mankind fell into a state of brokenness and sin—the repercussions of which have sent shockwaves throughout all of creation and time. For their own protection (and as we'll see, that of a future Savior), God had to drive Adam and Eve from the garden of Eden. God then appointed a cherubim with a flaming sword at the entrance back into Eden to "guard the way to the tree of life" (Genesis 3:24).

For a time, the Creator would be separated from his image-bearers. The narrow, blocked entry into Eden would foreshadow a narrow, unblocked entry back to heaven for future generations who would descend from Adam and Eve. There was only one way into Eden then, just as there is only one way into heaven now. His name is Jesus.

John 14:6—I am the way and the truth and the life. No one comes to the Father except through me.

Eden was where the fall occurred, but it was also the place where redemption began. God provided animal skins for Adam and Eve (Genesis 3:21), indicating that innocent creatures had to die to cover their sin. Though sin put separation between God and man, a redemptive theme began immediately at the fall and was progressively unveiled all through Scripture. This theme begins in Genesis and finds its ultimate fulfillment in the book of Revelation. Not only did God provide animal skins that pointed toward redemption, he provided the first prophecy about the one who would secure that redemption! This single prophecy is the key that explains the main story arc of the biblical narrative. It is the breakthrough detail I alluded to in the opening paragraphs of this chapter.

The First Messianic Prophecy

In theological circles, the verse at the opening of this chapter (Genesis 3:15) is known as the *protoevangelium*. The Greek *proto* means "original," and *evangelion* is the word for "good news." In Latin, it is translated *evangelium*. Genesis 3:15 is the original good news, or the first promise of a future redeemer—one who would defeat the guardian serpent-cherub.

In this prophecy, the future redeemer is called the "offspring" (NIV) or the "seed" (NASB) of the woman. This is the only verse in Scripture where a woman is said to have "seed." It is the Hebrew word *zara* (zaw-rah), applied elsewhere in Scripture only to males or in an agricultural seed-planting context. This is an early indication that the Savior would be born of a virgin without any human male DNA.

Notice the offspring is a *he*, and according to the prophecy, *he* will be wounded—but ultimately, *he* will crush the head of Satan. From the moment this prophecy was given, the enemy's primary goal was to eliminate the lineage of the future redeemer in order to keep God's prophecy from being fulfilled. If successful, this would have saved Satan's own head from being metaphorically crushed, made God a liar, and brought Satan one step closer to stealing God's throne—or so he thought.

This single prophecy explains so much in Scripture and makes previously confusing events suddenly make crystal-clear sense. In essence, Satan declared a seed-war. He was driven by a constant obsession with destroying anything or anyone who might lead to the birth and ministry of the promised offspring of the woman.

The Seed War

Genesis 3:15 is the first prophecy of a future Savior. Additional details about this Savior would be revealed as time moved forward and as God breathed more of Scripture into existence. From Genesis 3:15 onward, each time God

provided more prophetic details about the promised Messiah (seed of the woman), Satan would tighten his focus based on the additional information. Satan is not omniscient (or omnipotent, or omnipresent for that matter), and therefore he has had to study prophecy in his attempt to understand God's next move.

Whenever God issued a decree or promise related to the future Savior, Satan would zero in on the new details like a heat-seeking missile. Once you understand this concept, the spiritual warfare going on behind the scenes from Genesis chapter 3 all the way to the cross makes tremendous sense.

Here are several ways that the enemy's focus has narrowed with each new phase of God's plan being revealed. Each event cited below is directly related to Satan's activity behind the scenes as he learned new prophetic information related to the lineage, location, or timing of God's unfolding plan for the promised "seed of the woman."

THE NARROWING FOCUS OF THE SEED WAR

- The murder of Abel in Genesis 4
- Corruption of Adam's line in Genesis 6 (more on this in the next chapter)

- Plans to kill Abraham, from whom the Messiah would come (see Genesis 12 and 20)

- Extreme famine in the land of Canaan (Genesis 50)

- Destruction of the male Hebrew line in Exodus 1

- Pharaoh's change-of-mind pursuit in Exodus 14

- The populating of Canaan with corrupted beings (similar to Genesis 6) (see Genesis 15 and Joshua 2–12)

- Multiple attacks on David's line (see below) based on 2 Samuel 7:12 (and surrounding)

- Haman's nearly successful plan to kill all Jewish people in Esther 3

- Joseph's fears in Matthew 1

- Herod's murder of all males under the age of two in Matthew 2

- The temptation of Jesus in Luke 4:1-13

- The attempt to throw Jesus off a cliff in Luke 4:28-29

- Two violent storms on the sea (which caused even seasoned fisherman to feel hopeless) (see Mark 4 and Luke 8)

- The crucifixion of Jesus

Each time the enemy thought he had God cornered, Yahweh demonstrated his flawlessly omniscient and masterful planning. Every time the enemy was about to say, "Checkmate," the great "I AM" would unveil a surprise game-changing move that would lead Satan closer to his own ultimate failure and judgment.

Whenever Satan thought he was on the verge of eliminating the line of the Messiah, God would flip the script, leaving him completely emptyhanded. This process was repeated down through the biblical ages until, finally, Satan could almost taste the win when a bloody, beaten Jesus hung on a gruesome Roman cross.

However, the age-old enemy would soon learn that what he thought was a long-awaited windfall was actually his own undoing. The resurrection of Jesus Christ was the greatest knockout counterpunch in world history. Jesus's heel had been bruised, but in that same moment, the serpent's head had been delivered a death blow. The great dragon—that serpent of old—thought he finally had the offspring of the woman where he wanted him, only to find he helped fulfill the very prophecy he had spent thousands of years trying to usurp.

The Enemy's Strategy Shift

I've been told by nature guides and outdoorsmen that the severed head of a poisonous snake can still bite, and that 22-24 hours after death, some snakes can still coil tightly around an arm if picked up. Though Satan's head has been crushed, he still has venom. Although he is as good as dead, he is not yet in his place of eternal judgment. That future moment is surely coming, but at the current time his crushed head still bites and his body still coils violently.

Satan's seed-war campaign was an abysmal failure at every turn. The promised redeemer had come and succeeded against all odds. The image-bearing humans could now be reconciled to their Creator. Satan's death blow would require time to take effect. Two thousand years after the resurrection, he still roams—for a season. After his head-crushing defeat at the cross, the enemy's focus would have to shift in order to do as much damage as possible until his prophesied end.

Beginning with the resurrection, Satan's focus shifted from keeping the promised Messiah from coming, to destroying the church and the Jewish people. The enemy's goal now is to keep end-time prophecies (including his own judgment) from being fulfilled. This is why the church and Jewish people have suffered more persecution and martyrdom than any other groups of people throughout the church age. In fact, they are the two most persecuted people groups—by far—in our day.

In addition to this strategy, Satan has also been laying the groundwork for the future seven-year period known as the tribulation period, or the day of the Lord. Once again, he has studied prophecy to see what is coming and how he can attempt to leverage it to his advantage. In his own self-deception, he still thinks he can find a way to win—to avoid eternal death. Satan is hard at work with new plans to war against the Creator in the last days—plans that are doomed to fail, though Satan and deceived humans will still attempt to carry them out.

There is one key detail in Genesis 3:15 that I have not covered in this chapter because it deals specifically with events that will occur during the future tribulation period. We'll talk about this final phase of Satan's reworked plans in chapter 18. But first I'd like to take you on a more detailed tour of something I mentioned briefly earlier—the corrupting of all human flesh in Genesis chapter 6. Turn the page, and we'll study some little-known but clearly presented reasons for the flood of Noah's day and how all this relates to spiritual warfare.

CHAPTER 4

Genesis 6 and the Pre-Flood World

The Nephilim were on the earth in those days, and also afterward, when the sons of God came in to the daughters of men, and they bore children to them. Those were the mighty men who were of old, men of renown.

GENESIS 6:4 (NASB)

God looked on the earth, and behold, it was corrupt; for all flesh had corrupted their way upon the earth.

GENESIS 6:12 (NASB)

I love designing characters, and it takes years of practice and learning to become an expert character designer. I'm not there yet. When I say expert, I think of some of the people I've met who work in the animated feature film industry. I've met some master character designers from Disney, Pixar, Sony Animation, and a few other major studios. They eat, sleep, and breathe character design. They have natural talent, but they have also put in the necessary work to become masters of their craft. As with any skill, practice makes perfect—or in this case, better.

When I look at my sketchbooks from 15 or 20 years ago, I notice that my early character designs lack personality and they feel somewhat rigid and lifeless. I've gotten better over the years and there's one concept in particular that has helped give my drawings more life and energy. It's known as line of action. It's actually a very simple concept: Before you rough out a character pose, think about the direction of action in the pose.

The goal of the line of action is to gain a sense of weight and movement—making the pose more dynamic. I learned that if you simply sketch a line of action in the appropriate curve and direction in which you want the sense of energy to go, then design your character around this line of action, it automatically breathes life into the pose. A line of action adds clarity and purpose to a pose, making it much more dynamic and understandable.

Once a character is animated on screen, you no longer see the line of action, but you sense it. The line of action from the initial sketched pose is long gone by the time the character is posed or animated on screen, but its weight and energy are still felt in the scene.

Similarly, there is a line of action in Genesis chapter 6 that adds weight and direction to the rest of Scripture. Perhaps you have never noticed this line of action, or maybe it seemed too strange or confusing to consider. The first four verses of Genesis 6 contain some of the strangest information given to us in Scripture. Many people breeze over these verses as an odd record about a confusing ancient event, not realizing any connection to other portions of the Bible.

These are not obscure throwaway verses. The opening section of Genesis 6 is vital to understanding God's judgment in Noah's day, the conquest of Canaan, and possibly some events that will take place during the future tribulation period. Remember that 2 Timothy 3:16 boldly proclaims that *all* Scripture is God-breathed—including the opening verses of Genesis chapter 6. Now, get ready for a very unusual discussion.

2 Timothy 3:16-17—All Scripture is God-breathed and is useful for teaching, rebuking, correcting and training in righteousness, so that the servant of God may be thoroughly equipped for every good work.

The Genesis 3 and Genesis 6 Connection

In the previous chapter, we studied the connection between Genesis 3:15 and the ensuing activity of the enemy throughout the pages of Scripture. From Genesis 3:15 to the birth of Christ, Satan used several strategies to keep the promised offspring (or seed of the woman) from being born. One of these strategies during the pre-flood era was an attempt to corrupt Adam's lineage—to pollute the human genome. If the future seed of the woman was without a purely human woman from whom to come, then the prophesied future redeemer would not be able to arrive.

In Genesis 6, people tend to focus on the narrative beginning at verse 5, but the first four verses provide key details about what was occurring before the flood. They also connect the flood with Genesis 3:15, the post-flood conquest of Canaan, and perhaps even some events in the book of Revelation.[1]

QUICK FACT: DID YOU KNOW...

there are more than 200 myths from all over the world about a major flood? This points to a universal truth— that there was indeed a worldwide flood in the ancient past.

I'll cut to the chase and share an overview of what the first four verses of Genesis 6 describe. It's weird, so buckle up. A careful reading of Genesis 6 informs us that prior to the flood of Noah's day, the world was a very different place. After people multiplied quite a bit, fallen angels took women and mated with them— creating a hybrid race of beings. These half-angel, half-human creatures had extraordinary strength, great size, were very violent, and were well-known around the world.

Their physical makeup was distinctly different from what God had originally created. In modern terms, we would say their DNA was corrupted, and this was passed down to subsequent generations. See, I told you—weird. Was I right? Before I explain further, I want you to be aware that there are two main views of what took place here. Let's look at them briefly.

Two Vastly Differing Views

There are two key views about the identity of "the sons of God" in Genesis 6: The Sethite view, and the supernatural view. The Sethite view implies that Genesis 6 is simply saying that godly men who descended from Adam's son Seth married ungodly, worldly women, and their offspring led to more widespread sinful activity in the world. The supernatural view asserts that the Hebrew words used in the text make it clear that this was the union of heavenly beings with earthly, human women—and that their offspring formed a new hybrid race of beings known as the Nephilim.

When it comes to the stranger passages of Scripture, it is not uncommon for Bible teachers to look for an interpretation that is more palatable to modern sensibilities. But for those of us who believe in the inerrancy and accuracy of Scripture, the goal is always to let the original words of the text explain their true meaning. Like other portions of Scripture, Genesis 6 is not difficult to understand per se, but the information in it may be difficult for some to accept. Allowing Scripture to speak for itself is key to understanding difficult or confusing sections of the Bible.

Understanding Genesis 6

With that in mind, let's take a closer look at the first four verses (and a few others) of Genesis 6. I'll include some Hebrew word meanings and a bit of commentary so you get a better idea of what this passage is saying. What follows is a bit technical, and the inclusion of the root word explanations and some commentary won't allow the Scripture text to flow as smoothly or poetically as it normally would, but I think the inserted words and definitions will prove helpful for us to more fully understand what exactly is going on here. Furthermore, I believe these explanations will help clarify why all this is important to the topic of spiritual warfare and the seed war that we've been discussing. I would encourage you to take some time to read through the following passages slowly. Then I'll unpack them a bit in the paragraphs that follow.

Genesis 6:1-4

> Now it came about, when men began [*hechel* = began to pollute, defile, or profane] to multiply [*larov* = to become great in number] on the face of the land, and daughters were born to them, that

the sons of God [*venei haelohim* = direct heavenly creations of God; that is, angelic beings] saw that the daughters of men were beautiful; and they took wives for themselves, whomever they chose. Then the LORD said, "My Spirit shall not strive with man forever, because he also is flesh; nevertheless his days shall be one hundred and twenty years." The Nephilim [*hannefilim* = two distinct groups of fallen beings, one before the flood and one after the flood; root word *naphal* = to fall] were on the earth in those days, and also afterward, when the sons of God [*venei haelohim* = direct heavenly creations of God; that is, angelic beings] came in to the daughters of men [notice the distinction: a union of heavenly males and human females], and they bore children to them. Those were the mighty men [*haggibborim* = overly powerful beings/giants, root word *gabar* = magnified, arrogantly stronger] who were of old [*meovlam* = from antiquity, from early on], men [*anshei* = mighty men of high degree] of renown [*hashem* = famous or well-known] (NASB).[2]

Genesis Chapter 6:11-13

Now the earth was corrupt [*vattishachet* = depraved behavior, polluted, blemished; root word *shachath* = perhaps to go to ruin] in the sight of God, and the earth was filled with violence. God looked on the earth, and behold, it was corrupt [root word *shachath* = perhaps to go to ruin]; for all flesh had corrupted [root word *shachath* = perhaps to go to ruin] their way upon the earth. Then God said to Noah, "The end [*ketz* = end, the furthest border] of all flesh [*basar* = bodies, flesh, meat] has come before Me; for the earth is filled with violence because of them; and behold, I am about to destroy them with the earth (NASB).

It is clear from the original Hebrew words in Genesis 6 that it was angelic beings who mated with human women, creating a new type of being characterized by great strength, size, and violent dispositions, who in turn further corrupted all flesh (humans and animals alike) to the point where all of God's creatures had become corrupted "to the furthest border"—to borrow the meaning from one of the words above—almost beyond repair. Apparently Noah and his family were among the few humans left who were both right with God and still 100 percent human, and the animals God led to the ark still had uncorrupted DNA.

I should note that one alternate detail related to the supernatural view held by some theologians sees the fallen angels as being disembodied rather than having physical bodies. That view asserts that disembodied fallen angels possessed willing males to impregnate women to create the hybrid offspring (as opposed to the fallen angels being physical in nature and possessing some type of seed of their own).

In my opinion, this view does not answer how a new type of being (the Nephilim) would be produced. We know angels do not marry (Matthew 22:30), but this does not necessarily mean they do not have seed (male sperm, or some fallen-angel equivalent). We're told in Genesis 3:15 that Satan has "seed" or a way to produce offspring. Theologians vary on what this means exactly, but it seems to lend credence to the idea that, at least for a time, it was possible for angelic beings to mate with human women.

Jude 6-7 speaks of these Nephilim-producing angels as having left their "proper dwelling" to commence their mischief. This could mean they somehow left their angelic body to become disembodied, or that they somehow left their natural unseen heavenly realm to occupy the physical realm. In the first case, they would need to possess human males (but this doesn't answer how angelic DNA would have mixed with human DNA). In the second case, they would have directly mated with human women. I cautiously, humbly, and loosely lean toward this second view.

Admittedly, this is a highly debated subject even among theologians and Bible prophecy experts. Scripture is not 100 percent clear on the details, so we must be very careful in our approach and cautiously resist engaging in speculation.

As always, we should study the full breadth of Scripture in order to understand a confusing or debated passage more fully. As we allow Scripture to interpret Scripture, we gain a more complete picture of how various passages in the Bible line up. With this in mind, there are two passages in the New Testament that shed further light on the activity described in Genesis 6. As standalone passages, these are confusing, but in light of what we've just studied, they make tremendous sense.

Jude 6-7

> The angels who did not keep their positions of authority but abandoned their proper dwelling—these he has kept in darkness, bound with everlasting chains for judgment on the great Day. In a similar way, Sodom and Gomorrah and the surrounding towns gave themselves up to sexual immorality and perversion. They serve as an example of those who suffer the punishment of eternal fire.

2 Peter 2:4-6

> …if God did not spare angels when they sinned, but sent them to hell, putting them in chains of darkness to be held for judgment; if he did not spare the ancient world when he brought the flood on its ungodly people, but protected Noah, a preacher of righteousness, and seven others; if he condemned the cities of Sodom and Gomorrah by burning them to ashes, and made them an example of what is going to happen to the ungodly.

Notice the similarities in both accounts. Both speak of angels who left their original state and rebelled. Both passages also mention the flood of Noah's day and the destruction of Sodom and Gomorrah. In the Noah account, women were impregnated by angelic beings (Genesis 6:4). In the Sodom and Gomorrah account, men wanted to rape angelic beings (Genesis 19:1-5). I apologize for the graphic nature of what is described here, but this is indeed what Scripture teaches.

AWKWARD!

By studying the full context of Scripture, we can deduce that the supernatural view of Genesis 6 is biblically accurate. The flood judgment wasn't just to punish sin, but also to preserve the humanness of mankind so the future Savior could still arrive as the offspring of the woman. Do you see the connection?

This is admittedly a very difficult topic to understand and Genesis 6 can be a divisive portion of Scripture because people interpret it in different ways. We can know, however, that according to Matthew 22:30, angels do not marry. But apparently long ago in the past, certain fallen angels "left their first estate" and had the ability to procreate. We're not given enough information to understand all the details of how this took place, but Genesis 6:1-4 (and the support from Jude and 2 Peter) is clear on the fact that it did indeed occur. This seems to have been a one-time event that God put a stop to.

We see this "one-time event" pattern in the original fall of Satan along with one-third of the angels, in Genesis 6, and again at the Tower of Babel. Each rebellion seemed to have found a "loophole" that was then closed afterward. By loophole, I don't mean to imply God was not aware of what would happen. He is completely sovereign and knows all things past, present, and future. Though we don't have all the information to understand what took place in Genesis 6, we must trust the clear words of Scripture for what we do know to have happened.

QUICK FACT: DID YOU KNOW...

that ancient cultures from every continent where people lived recorded stories of violent hybrid giant creatures and a massive flood judgment? Why would various ancient cultures—most of which never crossed paths with each other—all contain stories of violent hybrid giants and a great flood unless there was a central truth to the story? For example, such stories exist in Celtic, Greek, Roman, Hindu, Norse, Native American (North and South America), Pacific Islanders, and Aboriginal Australian mythology.

Now It All Makes Sense

There is another perplexing set of circumstances in Scripture that makes sense in light of what we've learned from Genesis 6. Critics of the Bible and Christianity have often cited God's seemingly genocidal commands to Joshua and the Israelites to annihilate entire people groups while conquering the Promised Land. We also find scriptural references about giants inhabiting the Promised

Land prior to (Numbers 13:32-33) and during (Joshua chapters 2–12) the conquest of Canaan. The question is, how are these two connected, and how does Genesis 6 unlock the mystery?

There is an easily overlooked phrase in Genesis 6:4 that informs us that Nephilim were on the earth in those days (before the flood)—"and also afterward." Does that mean there were still Nephilim after the flood? Yes. They showed up again during conquest of Canaan. Remember when Moses sent the spies in to check out the Promised Land? In Numbers 13:32-33, we read, "They spread among the Israelites a bad report about the land they had explored. They said, 'The land we explored devours those living in it. All the people we saw there are of great size. We saw the Nephilim there (the descendants of Anak come from the Nephilim). We seemed like grasshoppers in our own eyes, and we looked the same to them.'" While their report was likely exaggerated (stating that "all" the people were giants), it caused the people to become fearful, and dissension spread through them all. In the end, they failed to trust God for victory over the Canaanites.

The added information stating that the descendants of Anak came from the Nephilim should be duly noted. The Anakim were a race of giant warriors who lived in the land of Canaan (see Deuteronomy 2:10,21; 9:2; Joshua 15:13; 14:15; 21:11). According to Numbers 13:33, they came from the Nephilim. Again, keep in mind that these details describe a post-flood era.

There are various views regarding how the Nephilim were reintroduced after the flood, and volumes of books have been written on the topic. Some say Noah's son Ham's line had hidden Nephilim DNA present (through Ham's wife). Some posit that certain Nephilim survived the flood (but in my opinion, this theory does not square with the clear teaching in Genesis 7:21-23 that every single earthly creature outside of the ark died in the flood). Some say what took place during the post-flood Tower of Babel events with Nimrod somehow reintroduced a form of Nephilim back into the world. This is the scenario I lean toward (and will unpack further in the next chapter), although I don't think anyone can be dogmatic about this.

There are also some Bible scholars who point out that the spies, in their attempt to discourage the Israelites, likely exaggerated when they made reference to the Nephilim. In giving their report, they were being disobedient to God, which may indicate that what they said probably wasn't trustworthy.

Ultimately, there simply is not enough clear information to arrive at a conclusion. Yet for a historical understanding of spiritual warfare through the ages, this is still a fact worthy of note.

The question now is, Why did the post-flood Nephilim populate Canaan? As we study Scripture, we find the answer—and ultimately it is related to the seed war mentioned in the prophecy in Genesis 3:15. In Genesis 15, God laid out his covenant with Abraham and included a key time frame. In verse 13 we read, "The LORD said to him, 'Know for certain that for four hundred years your descendants will be strangers in a country not their own and that they will be enslaved and mistreated there.'"

As some prophecy experts have said, this gave Satan 400 years to lay a minefield. In his efforts to thwart the arrival of the promised Messiah, Satan paid close attention to each prophecy given. With each new bit of prophetic information, Satan grew more specific in his tactics. In this case, it appears that Satan used his influence over the fallen world to place powerful, nonhuman Nephilim in the very same land God had promised to Abraham. Then 400-plus years of DNA-corrupting, Nephilim-infused population explosion filled and polluted the Promised Land.

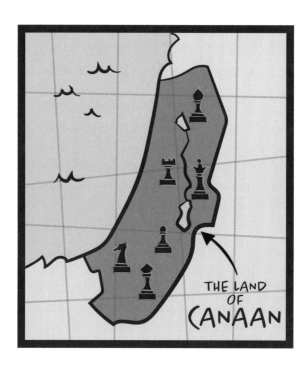

Again, this area of study—even among prophecy students—is full of debate. It is a secondary issue for sure, but one worth studying to better understand the nature of spiritual warfare. I have seen prophecy students focus too much on the topic, making assumptions and assertions that the Bible simply does not state. On the other end of the spectrum, I've seen people completely ignore the facts presented above and act as if the topic doesn't even exist in the pages of Scripture. I hope that what I have presented above is a healthy, balanced, Bible-centered approach to the topic and I encourage you to study it further for yourself—with caution. We should allow the Bible to speak for itself, no matter how strange or foreign a topic might be to our modern sensibilities. And we should be careful not to sensationalize topics or read our own thoughts and ideas into Scripture.

Fallen Angels vs. Demons

While the events of Genesis 6 took place long ago, there are some implications for us today. In the context of spiritual warfare, there are a few details theologians differ on depending on their view of Genesis 6. Some refer to all fallen angels as demons. In their mind, these two terms refer to the same beings. Other theologians make a distinction between demons and fallen angels.

The second group points out that demons (also called unclean spirits in Scripture) always seem to desire to inhabit humans, whereas fallen angels already possess the ability to take on physical characteristics. The Bible confirms that both holy and fallen angels can move between realms (Genesis 19; Hebrews 13:2).

This second group of theologians posit that the demons who desire to inhabit human bodies are the disembodied spirits of the Nephilim. They desire to once again experience physicality, whereas fallen angels do not attempt to inhabit humans because they already have the ability to manifest themselves physically in the earthly realm.

A third possibility exists as well: It could be that some fallen angels can materialize interdimensionally while others cannot. Perhaps some lower-ranking fallen angels can't pierce the veil and therefore attempt their mischief via possessing humans when the option is available to them. I do not yet have a firm conviction about which of these views is correct, but I present them here so you can be aware of the varying perspectives. My opinion at this time is that Scripture simply does not provide a crystal-clear answer, and I would much rather err on the side of caution than make a definitive statement. After all, if God has chosen to hide certain types of information from us, we can be certain there is a good reason for that.

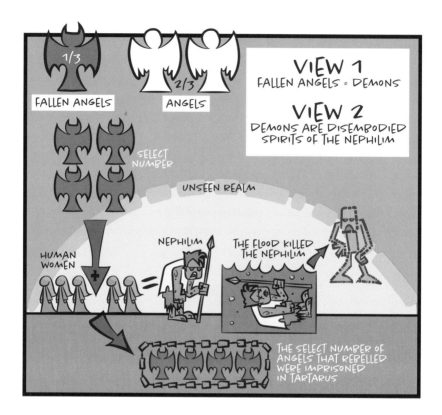

Some prophecy experts submit that if any so-called aliens or UFOs are indeed real, that they are likely fallen angels preparing a great end-times deception. In my opinion, this is plausible because the enemy knows that a false narrative will be needed after the rapture occurs to explain why Christians have all disappeared from the earth. As I've mentioned, Scripture does support the fact that angels can move between realms and possess real physical properties. We also see in the Bible that angels may also have what appear to be vehicles and some type of dual-realm technology (See 2 Kings 2:11-12; Ezekiel 1:15-21; Revelation 8:5; 9:7-9).

If at this point the topics in this chapter still feel too strange for you to consider, that's okay. Table the information for now and keep reading. My goal is to provide as much information as I can related to the connection between our physical world and the unseen realm so that when we study Ephesians 6 and the spiritual armor available to every believer (beginning in chapter 10), you will have a breadth of foundational information to rely on. With that said, get ready for one more strange chapter.

CHAPTER 5

Babylon Revisited

When the Most High assigned lands to the nations, when he divided up the human race, he established the boundaries of the peoples according to the number in his heavenly court.

DEUTERONOMY 32:8 (NLT)

My first mission trip was to Brazil in 1994. I had taken a couple of Spanish classes in college, but I spoke zero Portuguese—the official language of Brazil. Many of the Brazilians we came to know spoke some Spanish as well, so we used that bridge-building language as our means of communication when our interpreter wasn't around.

Fast-forward to more recent years, and I've faced quite a different scenario. In the recent past, I've been on mission trips to the Dominican Republic and Haiti. In the D.R., the people speak Spanish, but in Haiti, the common language

is Haitian Creole. We were fortunate enough to have interpreters on these trips, but we also had apps on our mission-trip-equipped smart devices that helped tremendously when the interpreters were busy. These new game-changing tools helped break down the language barrier so we could communicate more easily with the people we were serving.

In this chapter, I want to break down the language barrier in a slightly different way, and here's what I mean. Many believers assume the biblical account of the Tower of Babel is merely a standalone narrative about God confusing human speech so the people wouldn't finish an ancient skyscraper. On the other hand, skeptics view this record in Genesis 11 as a mythological bedtime story used by pre-enlightenment people to explain why there are so many languages in the world today. Here, I want to *break down* (see what I did there?) what was really going on before God confused the languages in that strangely fascinating record of Genesis 11.

Pulling Back the Curtain

Believe it or not, the record of what happened at Babel is not a standalone story, but one that has had influence through the ages since, continues to have an effect on culture today, and will culminate in the future tribulation period as detailed in the book of Revelation. There was a broader purpose to the events that took place at Babel—one that connects it to the events we've been studying in Genesis chapters 3 and 6.

BRUEGEL'S PAINTING

In my book *The Non-Prophet's Guide™ to the Book of Revelation*, I detailed the history of Babylon beginning with the original events that took place at Babel. In that work, the purpose was to show the background and long history of Babel's influence and how it related to Revelation chapters 17 and 18, which detail the complete collapse of end-times Babylon and the Babylonian system that will exist during the seven-year tribulation period. Here is an excerpt from that chapter that details the purpose of Babel and how its influence has morphed and remained throughout world history:

- Babylon shows up in two key forms in the Old Testament. First, in a man-centered, God-defying religious form seen in the account of Nimrod and the Tower of Babel (Genesis 11). Second, around 1,650 years later we read about Babylon again, this time as a wealthy conquering political form under Nebuchadnezzar…[1]

- The first we hear of Babylon in Scripture is in the account detailed in Genesis 11. There, we read about how Nimrod—a descendant of Noah—developed an anti-God religion and leveraged his influence to build a city and a tower that was designed to reach heaven…There was a lot more going on here than just a rebellious man with aspirations to build a skyscraper tall enough to pierce heaven's zip code [and avoid another potential future judgment via rising floodwaters]. This was an attempt to build a global political and religious system in rebellion against God. It was a satanically led merging of technology, human-centered occult religion, and global government.

NEBBY

- On a much smaller scale, there is a sense in which that's what people try to do today when they use an Ouija board or consult with a medium. *Babylon* means "gateway to god" or "the gateway to the gods." Several times in Scripture, fallen angels are referred to as lowercase-*g* gods. At the Tower of Babel, man and evil entities were attempting to work together through the veil that separates the seen and unseen realms in open defiance against the Lord [knowing this rebellion would incur God's judgment].[2]

Here's where things get interesting:

- History informs us that Nimrod had a wife named Semiramis. Before marriage, she had a son named Tammuz, whom she claimed was supernaturally placed in her womb, this making him a savior child born of a virgin.

- Ancient stories about Tammuz say he was gored by a boar, died, was dead for 40 days, then came back to life. Sound familiar? Again, Satan is always the master (but twisted) counterfeiter. Based on the prophecy in Genesis 3:15 of a future virgin-born Savior, Satan was attempting to place his chess piece on the board with early plans to deceive the world. Semiramis and Tammuz came to be worshipped, and Semiramis came to be known as "the Queen of Heaven."

- As history marched forward, the same basic counterfeit-gospel story (virgin mother, savior baby killed and resurrected) and the immoral occult practices have proliferated in various key empires around the world. Only the names have changed.

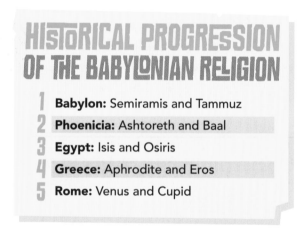

HISTORICAL PROGRESSION OF THE BABYLONIAN RELIGION

1 **Babylon:** Semiramis and Tammuz
2 **Phoenicia:** Ashtoreth and Baal
3 **Egypt:** Isis and Osiris
4 **Greece:** Aphrodite and Eros
5 **Rome:** Venus and Cupid

- The subsequent iterations of the pair ended in Rome, but remember, a Roman Empire of sorts (along with all that goes with it) will spring to life at the time of the antichrist. The closer we get to this time, the more stagesetting we should expect to see.[3]

So when God scattered the nations, he wasn't stifling progress, interrupting ingenuity, or discouraging entrepreneurialism. He was keeping Nimrod and his cohorts from doing something very specific. Nimrod may have been colluding with fallen angels to form a false global religion and a rebellious global government.

Based on a study of Deuteronomy 4:16-20, it seems that when God responded to the rebellion at the Tower of Babel and separated mankind into nations

(Genesis 10:25; 11:1-9), certain fallen angels became associated with specific territories. As we study Scripture, we find that throughout ancient history, the various nations worshipped fallen angels through pagan idolatry. Yet in this strange scenario, God kept the people of Israel for his own—and through them would come the long-awaited Messiah.

Historical records tell us that many pagan practices were incorporated into ancient Roman culture. Later, when secret societies emerged and multiplied during the second century AD, the Romans often incorporated various aspects of ancient Babylonian occult practices into these societies. In like manner, the closer we get to the end of the church age, the more prominent, bold, and mainstream the occult will become in modern society. The New Testament cites an end-times increase in occult-influenced globalist ideology that will find its full effect during the tribulation period after the rapture of the church. And we can trace it all back to Babel, where God confused the languages and scattered the people.

A Closer Look at Nimrod

In the previous chapter, where I highlighted a few of the different views about how the Nephilim reemerged after the flood, I mentioned that we would take a closer look at the topic in this chapter. One possibility with some biblical support is that Nimrod may have—through some kind of interaction with fallen angels—discovered or developed the means by which post-flood people could become like the Nephilim. I know this may sound like the plot to a far-fetched Marvel Comics movie, but let's look at the biblical evidence. I'm not adamant about this particular take on Nimrod, but—as you'll see below—I believe there is some textual support for it in the Bible.

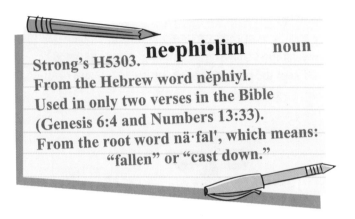

ne•phi•lim   noun

Strong's H5303.
From the Hebrew word nĕphiyl.
Used in only two verses in the Bible
(Genesis 6:4 and Numbers 13:33).
From the root word nä·fal', which means:
"fallen" or "cast down."

In Genesis 10, we find the passage known to theologians as the Table of Nations. This genealogical record of the descendants of Noah and his sons also provides short sections of additional information. This is where we can learn more about Nimrod and his "gateway to the gods" than we do in Genesis 11, which documents the Tower of Babel account—especially if we do a bit of digging into the original Hebrew text.

In Genesis 10:8-12, we read,

> Cush was the father of Nimrod, who *became a mighty warrior* on the earth. He was a *mighty hunter before the* Lord; that is why it is said, "Like Nimrod, a *mighty hunter before the* Lord." The first *centers of his kingdom* were Babylon, Uruk, Akkad and Kalneh, in Shinar. From that land he went to Assyria, where he built Nineveh, Rehoboth Ir, Calah and Resen, which is between Nineveh and Calah—which is the great city (emphasis added).

In addition to discovering that Nimrod was Noah's great-grandson (from Noah's son Ham's genealogical line), we learn some other insightful information.

NIMROD

First, however, I'd like to give you a heads-up about the next six paragraphs, which are a bit technical. But if you'll bear with me, I think you'll walk away with a greater appreciation of what was likely going on at the Tower

of Babel—and how it relates to spiritual warfare. Now, back to your regularly scheduled Scripture analysis.

In Genesis 10:8, where we read, "Nimrod...became a mighty warrior," the original Hebrew text could be more literally rendered, "Nimrod was polluted/corrupted into a magnified/absolutely stronger, insolent being." Then in verse 9, where we read, "He was a mighty hunter before the LORD," the original Hebrew could be translated more literally, "He was a strengthened/increased being who mightily ensnared people into outright rebellion against God." The phrase "before the LORD" doesn't mean "in honor of God" or "in the view of God." It is a term of defiance. In our modern vernacular, it means "in God's face!"

The Hebrew word used in this passage for "mighty one" and "mighty hunter" is *gibbor*. It is the same word used in Genesis 6:4, which refers to the Nephilim as "mighty men" (NKJV). The difference in Nimrod's case is that somehow he *became* a mighty one.

Perhaps Nimrod and his evil cohorts were offering this means by which to become a mighty one to anyone who would join them. Supporting this theory is the fact that the Hebrew word *shem*—used for "men of renown" in Genesis 6:4 (describing the Nephilim)—is the very same word used in Genesis 11:4, where the Babel-builders said, "Let us...make *a name* for ourselves."

Shem has to do with becoming famous—but with negative connotations. In modern-day language, we would use the word *infamous*. In essence, what

they were saying was, "Let us become like the infamous and mighty Nephilim; otherwise, we won't get to finish what we started and we'll be scattered all over the earth." They knew that what they were doing would get a strong reaction from the Lord.

Then Genesis 10:10-12 goes on to list more details about Nimrod's globalist agenda that culminated in the construction of the Tower of Babel. In summary, we learn from these few short verses that Nimrod colluded with fallen angels, somehow became an enhanced and mighty being similar to the pre-flood Nephilim, and attempted to lead a global rebellion against God by trying to access the heavenly realm via forbidden means.

As stated earlier, another view is that Ham (the son of Noah and grandfather of Nimrod) married a wife who had Nephilim DNA. After careful consideration, my problem with this view is that if God's plan was to utterly destroy all traces of the Nephilim (which is why he chose to use a global flood), then God wouldn't have "accidentally" let some Nephilim DNA survive. To say that some Nephilim DNA "escaped" implies that God isn't fully sovereign over all things.

Again, keep in mind that both views (Nimrod becoming a Nephilim, or having leftover Nephilim DNA derived from his grandfather's wife) are speculative. The one that seems most feasible to me is that Nimrod became a Nephilim-type being via some new, previously unknown means in collusion with fallen angels. Given that we know so little, it's best to simply be aware of what Scripture says and not attempt to build any key theology around this.

While the whole matter of the Nephilim is foreign to our modern sensibilities and we don't understand all the implications of what occurred at the Tower of Babel, what we *can* know for certain is that God found it absolutely necessary to take drastic action—to divide the land (Genesis 10:25; 1 Chronicles 1:19), to confuse the languages (Genesis 11:7), and to separate or scatter the people (verse 8). Something was occurring at Babel that—if left unchecked—would have severe consequences. This was no small feat, and it was outright spiritual warfare against God himself.

I labor this point because it demonstrates at least one way that Nephilim 2.0 could have reemerged as part of Satan's continuing plot to corrupt the lineage that was to lead to the future Messiah. As I mentioned in the previous chapter, by the time Moses sent his special-ops team into Canaan to do some reconnaissance, Nephilim were said to have filled the land (Numbers 13:33) via various tribes of giants. This explains the various accounts of post-flood giants as well as God's instructions to Joshua to destroy entire populations in the land of Canaan. This was not a genocide of innocent humans—it was judgment from God upon a rampantly wicked people that was necessary to protect His plans, people, and the lineage of the future Messiah.

In Leviticus 18:20-30, God warned the Israelites that the people of Canaan had defiled themselves and the land through "detestable customs" (verse 30) such as abhorrent sexual immorality and the offering of child sacrifices to Molech, a false god. Many other evil practices are detailed for us in Deuteronomy 18:9-14.

That is why God determined it was necessary for the Canaanites to be wiped out—for the sake of preserving his people and the lineage of Messiah.

All of this sheds light on what we've been referring to as the seed war spoken of in Genesis 3:15: the reemergence of Nephilim after the flood, the conquest of Canaan, and—as we'll study in chapter 18—key events during the future tribulation period.

Babylon in the End Times

Nationalism vs. Globalism

As just demonstrated, God is a nationalist. He very purposefully divided people into separate nations. This balance of power keeps evil rulers in check and acknowledges that human nature was greatly affected by the fall of Adam and Eve. Every human since has been born with a sin nature. It is our natural bent. Left unchecked, fallen people always take a turn for the worse. Though lofty dreams of an earthly utopia pervade songs, movies, and worldly philosophies, there will be no perfect world government until the millennial reign of Christ after the seven-year tribulation period.

The globalist agenda of today involves the merging of nations, religions, and monetary systems into one central power base. The restraining influence of the Holy Spirit-indwelt believers (that is, the church) keeps this globalist agenda from succeeding in our day. But the moment the rapture occurs, all true believers—along with the indwelling Holy Spirit—will no longer hold this tide of evil back.

2 Thessalonians 2:6-7—Now you know what is holding him back, so that he may be revealed at the proper time. For the secret power of lawlessness is already at work; but the one who now holds it back will continue to do so till he is taken out of the way.

True Worship vs. Occult Practice

When the rapture occurs, the light of genuine worship and access to the throne of God through the prayers of believers will be gone. Darkness will quickly fill the void. The evil, sexual perversion, and drug use that is so prevalent in occult practice today will reach new heights. The wickedness that has been simmering under the surface will emerge in full force. Even in our day, it is becoming more mainstream as we near the end of the age.

In Revelation chapter 9—after 12 of the 21 judgments will have occurred during the future tribulation period—we find that the majority of the people at that time will still refuse to turn from the ancient evil practices of Babylon. In verse 21 we read, "Nor did they repent of their murders, their magic arts, their sexual immorality or their thefts."

The once-hidden but now-revealed globalist agenda continues to build behind the scenes. Like a pressurized geyser, it will burst forth once the restraining influence of the church is gone via the rapture. The long-lived and openly stated plans of various globalist groups and leaders will finally be achieved for a short, terrible seven-year period of time.

This long-awaited merge of governments, religions, and financial systems will quickly lead to hell on earth. Until then, *we* as the church need to continue to be salt and light as we slow the cultural decay and expose the lies of the enemy. We are a thorn in his side. This will be the case until the rapture removes the church. Then Babylon—in all of its fullness—will emerge on the world stage for its final act.

A Warning Against Pop-Culture Occult Practices

As believers in Christ, we must at least be aware of the dangers of the occult even though we may find it repulsive and frightening—with good reason. Scripture prophesies that the formerly prevalent occultic influences and practices of the past will return in the end times, and we're seeing the groundwork being laid for this today. The battleground is being prepared, and unfortunately, there are many in the church who are unaware of what's happening because they're unable to recognize the subtle ways in which occultic thinking may have affected them.

In our day, many who call themselves Christians have unknowingly taken part in occult practices. They don't realize that reading horoscopes, studying astrology, visiting psychics, practicing hypnotism, playing with Ouija boards, reading tarot cards, and having their palms read are all occult practices. These practices can—knowingly or unknowingly—open connections with the evil principalities, powers, and rulers of the darkness that Paul talks about in Ephesians chapter 6. Yet these activities are seen by many people as mere innocent curiosities. Hasbro, one of the largest toymakers in the world, offers a Ouija board to children ages eight and up. Let that sink in for a moment. The fact that it is called a game should send shivers down our spine.

If you are involved in any of these popular occult practices, stop immediately. Renounce them for what they are and pray against any influence that you may have opened yourself up to. I understand this may seem a bit scary—and it is. Evil is real. The

enemy is crafty. The church of today is largely uneducated to some of these evil schemes. That is why this book is so important. The good news is that if you have invited Christ to be your Savior and Lord, you have the Holy Spirit's help. You are marked. Sealed. Protected. You have the power of the Holy Spirit within you and you can take action against evil—not because of who you are, but because of whose you are. If you are a believer, you cannot be possessed by any evil beings. The Holy Spirit and evil spirits cannot reside in the same dwelling.

Now, if you are reading this and you have not yet accepted Christ as your Savior, now would be a great time. Romans 10:9-10 promises, "If you declare with your mouth, 'Jesus is Lord,' and believe in your heart that God raised him from the dead, you will be saved. For it is with your heart that you believe and are justified, and it is with your mouth that you profess your faith and are saved."

For a more complete explanation about how to receive Christ, pause here and go to the final chapter of this book. There, in chapter 19, you'll find the ABCs of salvation—a clear and simple way to understand what it means to receive Christ.

The Bible tells us that when we receive Christ as Savior and Lord, we literally become a new creation. What a great way to get a fresh start and untangle ourselves from the evil influences and dark practices of the world!

2 Corinthians 5:17—Therefore, if anyone is in Christ, the new creation has come: The old has gone, the new is here!

CHAPTER 6

Epic Battles in the Unseen Realm

The one who is in you is greater than the one who is in the world.

1 JOHN 4:4

The new missionary and his wife lay in the small hut built for them on the edge of a tropical field by the previously unknown people group. After spending two years earning the trust of tribal peoples via short-term mission trips, the missionary couple were finally accepted by the indigenous group. God's open door of ministry to this remote tribe in the heart of Papua New Guinea had brought them to this moment—the couple's first night in the middle of nowhere with nothing but Jesus, each other, the thick tropical air, and their thoughts.

As they lay there, the full weight of their new responsibilities suddenly hit the husband. Feeling overwhelmed, he also began to experience an unusual and immense fear—an encroaching darkness. Just then, a terrifying sound broke through the humid pitch-black air that hung over the field next to their hut. A shrill, otherworldly voice interrupted the soothing symphony of chirping tropical creatures with a loud screech. Though this place was hundreds of miles away from any English-speaking people, the voice spoke in perfect English as it yelled, "I know who you are! You are a servant of the Most-High God. You do not belong here!"

That is a true story from a 30-year missions veteran from an organization that brings the gospel to unreached tribal peoples around the world. Our church in Maryland supported him and held an annual missions conference, during which he would come and share his experiences. He told us that story about his

first night in the full-time field along with a few other spine-tingling accounts of overt spiritual warfare that took place during the early years of his ministry in Papua New Guinea.

Since then I have befriended a few other full-time missionaries who share similar stories—some of them so incredible that if I didn't hear the details firsthand, and if I didn't know the missionaries and their trustworthy character personally, I would probably think the stories were untrue. The more godless and undeveloped the region, the more overt the spiritual warfare that takes place. It is as simple as that.

I have also witnessed a few such instances of spiritual warfare myself on short-term mission trips to Brazil, the Dominican Republic, and Haiti—though nothing quite as sensational as those experienced by my full-time missionary friends. The enemy seems to prefer to stay hidden—otherwise, people will realize that the principalities, powers, and rulers of this dark age (as Paul puts it in Ephesians 6:12) are indeed real, and that the biblical accounts of dark and demonic activity are true.

In modern-day America, we don't typically witness overt spiritual warfare. There are enough other distractions to keep the masses lulled into unawareness without the enemy having to show his true colors. This allows him to lure people into seemingly harmless occult activities without them realizing how dangerous they are. It also allows him to keep his powers hidden until it suits his end-times game plan, when he will "perform great signs and wonders to deceive" (Matthew 24:24).

With the exception of first responders and those in a few other occupations that deal with the painfully evil underbelly of society, the average person in America isn't likely to see open spiritual warfare in our current culture. The enemy prefers to stay hidden in the shadows and influence people from the other side of the veil—like the dark and invisible puppet master that he is.

However, if you have the opportunity to engage in conversations with missionaries who have served in third-world countries or other places that are devoid of Christianity, I guarantee you'll hear a story or two about open spiritual warfare similar to what we see in the book of Acts. Any Christian pioneer attempting to bring the light of the gospel into long-held enemy territory is likely to bump into overt spiritual warfare.

If such stories make the hair on your neck stand up and send shivers down your spine, I understand. If that is the case, I want to encourage you with the powerfully simple words found in the verse at the opening of this chapter. If you are a Christian, Jesus resides in you, and "the one who is in you is greater than the one who is in the world" (1 John 4:4). Remember and meditate on that verse when you find yourself anxious. We'll talk about the authority of the believer more in chapter 9, but for now, let that verse encourage you if you find the subject of spiritual warfare scary. I would also like to caution you that although we as believers should understand our enemy and his tactics, we should not become overly concerned or preoccupied with him or what he can do. Instead, we should focus our mind on God and his ways.

> Philippians 4:8—Finally, brothers and sisters, whatever is true, whatever is noble, whatever is right, whatever is pure, whatever is lovely, whatever is admirable—if anything is excellent or praiseworthy—think about such things.

With that story as a modern-day lead-in, let's take a look at a few accounts of spiritual warfare that have been recorded for us in Scripture. By studying these, we can learn some key biblical facts about the nature of spiritual warfare in the context of God's overall plan of redemption. These insights can better help us as we take part in the very real battle going on behind the scenes. The more we know, the better equipped we are to understand the schemes of the enemy and how to align our thoughts, actions, and understanding with those of God.

Vignettes of the Battle
Job and the Tension Between Free Will and God's Sovereignty

In the book of Job—probably the earliest-written account in Scripture—we gain some insight into certain aspects of spiritual warfare. In addition to what we discovered earlier in this book regarding Satan's access to the divine council, we also learn a few other things.

QUICK FACT: DID YOU KNOW...
that although Job is probably the oldest record in Scripture, it contains a detailed proclamation of a future Redeemer and the resurrection of the dead in the end times? See Job 19:25-27.

For example, we discover that any oppression that the enemy desires to send our way comes only after it has been filtered through the sovereign hands of God. Though the enemy may think he's attacking us to fulfill his own agenda, God has a greater purpose in mind for us if he allows such attacks to occur. There is a tension between free will and God's sovereignty. We can't understand it fully in our humanness, but that is okay. We are not God.

We also learn from Job that the enemy does have the ability to influence things on earth from his position in the unseen realm. Specifically, we deduce from Job's account that Satan can influence weather events (1:19), the motives and actions of godless people (verse 15), supernatural phenomena (verse 16), and the physical health of people (2:7).

Gideon and the Fog of War

In Judges chapter 7, we read about a tactic God used to defeat the enemies of Israel. In verse 22, we learn that as Gideon and his small army obeyed God's instructions, the Lord caused an unexpected fear, then great confusion, to settle in the enemy camp—leading the men in the massive army to attack each other instead of Gideon's men. This supernatural fog-of-battle confusion allowed Gideon's small force of 300 to defeat the combined armies of the Midianites, Amalekites, and "all the other eastern peoples" who had "settled in the valley, thick as locusts" (Judges 7:12).

If you read the various battle accounts of the Six-Day War against Israel in 1967, it appears God used similar tactics to bring about a great victory for Israel in much the same fashion. The tiny nation was vastly outnumbered. Facing the combined military forces of Egypt, Syria, Jordan, and Iraq, most of the people in Israel braced for a second Holocaust. But God had other plans. Through the bravery of the tiny Israeli military and story after story of what could only be explained as divine intervention, Israel soundly defeated the overwhelming force that was coming against her in a mere six days!

The enemies of Israel were fraught with inexplicable communication breakdowns, random yet perfectly timed maneuvers by the underequipped Israeli military, battle confusion and fear that caused whole units to abandon their equipment, friendly fire casualties, and the like. The stories of David versus Goliath and Gideon's small army of 300 are often poetically cited when recalling the astonishing victory of Israel over her enemies in the Six-Day War—

as well as Israel's War of Independence in 1948.

There is a yet-future war that is detailed in Ezekiel 38 and 39, where God will once again providentially intervene on behalf of Israel. This time God will defeat Israel's enemies in an overtly supernatural fashion. Ezekiel details a future end-times war when the Jewish

CHART OF ISRAELI WARS SINCE 1948

1948–49: Israel's War of Independence

1956: Suez Crisis

1967: Six-Day War

1973: Yom Kippur War

1982: Lebanon War

2006: Second Lebanon War

nation will be invaded from her northern border by the combined forces of Russia, Iran, Turkey, Libya, Sudan, and a few other allies.

As the enemy forces attack, God will use the same friendly fire confusion tactic he employed during Gideon's battle and other more recent conflicts in Israel's

history. In the heat of the campaign, God will also cause widespread weapons failures to occur, and he will send along a great earthquake, rain, and hail. As if all that weren't enough, there will also be burning sulfur and a plague, which, according to details provided in Ezekiel 39:6,11-16, seems to indicate the effects of nuclear warfare.

As happened in the famous encounter between David and Goliath, when God's chosen people face overwhelming odds against their land and against God's prophetic declarations, you can be sure that he will intervene to protect the people that he calls the apple of his eye (Zechariah 2:8).

Elisha and Our Unseen Protectors

In 2 Kings we read an interesting account that momentarily pulls back the curtain for us to catch a glimpse of the hidden realm that exists right alongside of us. The king of Aram was at war with Israel and kept trying to attack, but the

Lord shared his every move with Elisha the prophet, who would then warn the king of Israel. Finally, the king of Aram learned of Elisha's prophetic gift and sent an army to attack him in a place called Dothan. The army surrounded the city at night, and when Elisha's servant saw the army, he—understandably—freaked out.

Second Kings 6:15-18 takes us to the scene:

> When the servant of the man of God got up and went out early the next morning, an army with horses and chariots had surrounded the city. "Oh no, my lord! What shall we do?" the servant asked. "Don't be afraid," the prophet answered. "Those who are with us are more than those who are with them." And Elisha prayed, "Open his eyes, LORD, so that he may see." Then the LORD opened the servant's eyes, and he looked and saw the hills full of horses and chariots of fire all around Elisha. As the enemy came down toward him, Elisha prayed to the LORD, "Strike this army with blindness." So he struck them with blindness, as Elisha had asked.

In this passage we catch a glimpse of how God's angels protect his children from the enemy forces in the unseen realm as well as the seen. My personal favorite phrase in this passage is "those who are with us are more than those who are with them." Knowing that God is the Lord of Hosts—that he protects his own as we are "sealed" until the day of redemption (Ephesians 1:13-14) and that two-thirds of the angels did not rebel against God—is incredibly encouraging.

Anytime we face spiritual warfare, those of us who know the Lord can say that "those who are with us are more than those who are with them." Aside from the ratio of fallen to unfallen angels, we still have the numbers on our side: One person plus God equals a majority. Romans 8:31 powerfully states, "What, then, shall we say in response to these things? If God is for us, who can be against us?" Indeed!

Daniel and Territorial Angels

In Daniel chapter 10, we learn some interesting details about the unseen realm while Daniel is fasting and praying. The angel was probably Gabriel, for this account concerns the Jewish people, and Gabriel was the angel who visited Daniel in chapter 9. This angel informed Daniel that he had been dispatched the moment Daniel began to pray, but that a fallen angel known as "the prince of the Persian kingdom" fought him for 21 days, delaying him from delivering his message.

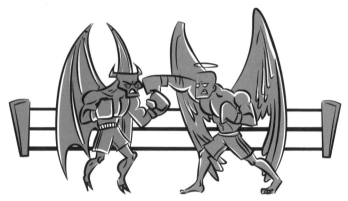

In verses 12-14 we read,

> Do not be afraid, Daniel. Since the first day that you set your mind to gain understanding and to humble yourself before your God, your words were heard, and I have come in response to them. But the prince of the Persian kingdom resisted me twenty-one days. Then Michael, one of the chief princes, came to help me, because I was detained there with the king of Persia. Now I have come to explain to you what will happen to your people in the future, for the vision concerns a time yet to come.

After physically strengthening Daniel, the angel informed the prophet that he would return to his paused battle with the prince of Persia (verses 20-21). The angel also mentioned that he was expecting to have to fight an additional foe—the prince of Greece. Then the angel (again, presumably Gabriel) reiterated that only Michael, the chief angel (or archangel) over Israel (verse 21), would be there to assist him in the fight. These details line up with our earlier assessment that when God divided the nations because of the Tower of Babel, powerful fallen angels obtained territorial oversight over specific regions. The details also support the idea that Gabriel is a prophetic messenger angel, and Michael is a warrior angel who protects Israel.

Speaking from a practical standpoint for us today, this provides insight into the fact that geopolitics, regional wars, and the like can be influenced by fallen angels and demons behind the scenes. We see the results in our daily newsfeed, but these verses (along with Ephesians 6, which we'll look at in the second half of this book) confirm that battles are going on in the unseen realm as well.

Jude and the Divine Legal System

In Jude, we read a single verse about a particular event mentioned nowhere else in Scripture. In verse 9 we read, "The archangel Michael, when he was disputing with the devil about the body of Moses, did not himself dare to condemn him for slander but said, 'The Lord rebuke you!'"

In essence, this passage tells us that Michael the archangel was in some kind of formal legal debate with Satan about the body of Moses after he died (Deuteronomy 34). It is important for us to note this formal system that seems to be set up in the unseen realm. We have bumped into it in the passages that cite the divine council, Satan's admission into said council, fallen angels having oversight of specific regions, etc.

This shouldn't surprise us given what we know about the nature of salvation. Scripture uses quite a bit of legal language when it comes to describing the concept of redemption. The transaction of our sin for Christ's righteousness is a legal one. Certain requirements had to be met for redemption to take place. The Old Testament law is full of meticulous legal and ceremonial details—all of which ultimately point to the redemption found in Jesus. These legal details and requirements beautifully point to grace as the means of our salvation. Jesus fulfilled the requirements, and his righteousness is imputed (a legal term) to us who believe in him.

We continue to see this legal framework in the symbolism found in the book of Revelation. The first set of judgments are what are known as the seal judgments.

The seven-sealed scroll depicted in the opening throes of the future tribulation period is depicted as a title deed to the earth—a legal document. The legalities regarding who had the authority to open the scroll, the order of the breaking of the seals, and the nature of what it all symbolized are very specific.

Somehow, even these end-time judgments will be a legally binding spiritual formality as Jesus methodically reclaims the earth. Scripture informs us that as we approach the end of the age, lawlessness will increase—culminating in global lawlessness and rebellion during the future tribulation period. In contrast, God's economy is marked by the solid structure of law and order.

The Special Ops Rapture Rescue

In 1 Thessalonians 4, we find the premiere section of Scripture regarding the future rapture of the church. The Greek word translated "rapture" is *harpazo*. This is the word used in 1 Thessalonians 4:17, which reads, "After that, we who are still alive and are left will be caught up [*harpazo*] together with them in the clouds to meet the Lord in the air. And so we will be with the Lord forever." As we study the 12 other uses of this Greek word in the New Testament, we can learn much more about the nature of this momentous future event.

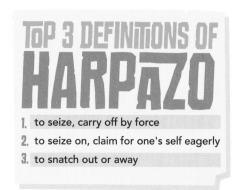

TOP 3 DEFINITIONS OF HARPAZO

1. to seize, carry off by force
2. to seize on, claim for one's self eagerly
3. to snatch out or away

EVERY USE OF HARPAZO IN THE NEW TESTAMENT

VERSE CONNOTATION

VERSE	CONNOTATION
Matthew 11:12	taken by violent force
Matthew 13:19	snatching away like a bird snatching a seed
John 6:15	to take by force
John 10:12	like a surprise snatching, as from a wolf
John 10:28	to snatch from an open hand without warning
John 10:29	to snatch from an open hand without warning
Acts 8:39	sudden disappearance/vanished from sight
Acts 23:10	urgently grabbed by a soldier and quickly taken away
2 Corinthians 12:2	suddenly caught up to heaven
2 Corinthians 12:4	suddenly caught up to heaven
1 Thessalonians 4:17	suddenly caught up into clouds
Jude 1:23	quickly rescuing someone from fire
Revelation 12:5	quickly snatched away from immediate danger

When you consider the definition of *harpazo* and carefully study its other uses, it becomes clear that this *harpazo* (what we refer to as the rapture) is a sudden, physical snatching away. What's more, there are several terms in 1 Thessalonians 4:16-18 (the Bible's primary rapture text) that are related to spiritual warfare. There we read of a "loud command," the "voice of the archangel" (probably Michael the war angel), and the "trumpet call of God." These terms all have warfare connotations.

This makes sense when you consider the fact that Satan is described as "the prince of the power of the air" (Ephesians 2:2 NKJV), "the god of this age" (2 Corinthians 4:4), "the ruler of this world" (John 14:30 NKJV), the ruler of "the kingdoms of this world" (Matthew 4:8), and, the deceiver "who leads the whole world astray" (Revelation 12:9). As a result of the fall, earth has been title-deeded to Satan. The future rapture of the church will be a heavenly special-ops snatch-and-grab invasion of enemy territory.

Notice that this seminal future event will take place in the clouds—right in the middle of the enemy territory of the prince of the power of the air. At the moment of the rapture, the spiritual warfare in the heavenly realm will invade our physical world unlike any other time in history. The current scientific theories of naturalism and uniformitarianism will be shattered in an instant when millions of Christians supernaturally disappear from earth via the *harpazo*.

This event will be like a divine D-Day. It will be a game-changing spiritual war event initiated by God himself, and it will set a whole series of events into motion—culminating in the utter defeat of enemy forces. Much like D-Day, the enemy knows this event is coming soon. He just doesn't know exactly when.

Unlike D-Day, the winning side will not experience any casualties. On the contrary, we will be more alive than we've ever been. The sacrifice has already been made by Jesus. Our spiritual salvation has been won. The D-Day-like rapture will complete the promise as our physical bodies are transformed to match our born-again spirits. "Therefore, encourage one another with these words" (1 Thessalonians 4:18). The second act of the two-part spiritual war event will occur at the end of the tribulation period when Jesus leads "the armies of heaven" (Revelation 19:14) in an all-out invasion to defeat the enemy and physically take back the earth.

Michael's Patience Pays Off

According to Revelation 12, at the midpoint of the future seven-year tribulation, a great battle will take place in the heavenly realm. As the judgments occur and Jesus is reclaiming the earth, there will come a time when Satan and his minions can no longer access the heavenly realm. No more accusing God's people before God's throne in the divine council. No more access to being "the prince of the power of the air." No more games. No more legal loopholes. Satan will be kicked out of heaven for good and relegated to earth until the end of the tribulation, when he will be bound for 1,000 years and, after that, cast into the lake of fire forever.

Though Michael the archangel had to respect rank and protocol when he debated Satan about the body of Moses, there will come a time when Michael finally gets to give Satan what's coming to him:

> Then war broke out in heaven. Michael and his angels fought against the dragon, and the dragon and his angels fought back. But he was not strong enough, and they lost their place in heaven. The great dragon was hurled down—that ancient serpent called the devil, or Satan, who leads the whole world astray. He was hurled to the earth, and his angels with him (Revelation 12:7-9).

What We Can Do

There are some practical takeaways from the various battle vignettes we've just read. These are accurate records from Scripture that give us insight into the nature of the war, the unfolding of the war, and ultimately, the end of the war. If you know Christ as Savior, you have joined the winning side. The outcome has already been settled. We need only to trust God's Word and fight the battle with the knowledge we gain as we study it. Here are a few principles we can apply:

- Job let us know that nothing can befall us unless it is first filtered through the sovereign and loving hands of the Father.

- Gideon and Elisha encouraged us with the knowledge that one person plus God is an unbeatable majority.

- Daniel helped us see that God immediately hears the sincere and humble prayers of his children. Though territorial enemy forces may disrupt things at times, God's plans will always be accomplished.

- Jude made it clear that, even in the unseen realm, the heavenly Father is a God of law and order—and that all lawlessness will one day be punished.

- Paul showed us how the future rapture of the church will be the supernatural event of the age we've all been waiting for—and that it will be perfectly timed.

- John shared his prophecy of the great dragon being soundly defeated by Michael the archangel in the greatest angelic prize fight in history. This should encourage us a great deal—knowing that one day, through overt spiritual warfare, God will level judgment against Satan, whose only contribution to history has been to steal, kill, and destroy (John 10:10).

SECTION 2:

TRAINING FOR BATTLE

CHAPTER 7

Making Sense of the Afterlife

Whoever has ears, let them hear what the Spirit says to the churches. To the one who is victorious, I will give the right to eat from the tree of life, which is in the paradise of God.

REVELATION 2:7

In 1995, Pixar's "overnight success" with *Toy Story*—their first theatrically released film—was 20 years in the making. The company had been on the verge of bankruptcy continually, even after partnering with Apple's Steve Jobs as their principal investor. The software company-turned-animation studio had a central leadership team of three people and an extended group of original director-animators. Together they made up what would come to be known as Pixar's brain trust.

This brain trust identified several things they didn't like about the animated films of their era and set out to blaze new trails in the animation industry. That they did—on many levels. Their initial string of uninterrupted record-breaking theatrical hits was unprecedented. The incredible success was due—in large part—to the key commitments developed and codified by that original brain trust.

HEY, ND...WHAT CAN YOU TELL US ABOUT THE BOTTOMLESS PIT?

THAT WAS THE NICKNAME MY MOM GAVE ME WHEN I WAS A TEENAGER. I STAYED HUNGRY FROM 8TH TO 10TH GRADE.

BIBLE COLLEGE & SEMINARY

EAST LIB

Among the key decisions were the following: There would be no singing characters; the well-known hero's journey story device would be passed like a baton to several characters in each film; films would stay in development until they truly found their center; storylines would not be dumbed down or overly simplified; the staff would make movies that they themselves would want to see; and story cohesion, including fully developed backstories, would be paramount.

These and other deliberate decisions are what led to Pixar's initial run of success. We are now 21 films into the life of the studio (at the time of this writing), and they still have not delivered a flop—though a few of their more recent films have been seen by critics as losing small bits of the Pixar touch.

A key reason for Pixar's success has been their films' broad audience appeal—they are watched by audiences young and old. The predictable storylines and cleanly executed outcomes of the average animated film of the day no longer satisfied people. Pixar's reaction to the overly simplified stories in animated films was to develop storylines that felt real and took risks. Within the fantasy realm of talking toys and monster worlds, the stories had real heart. They were developed with layered complexity and winding themes, broken expectations and unexpected twists. Moviegoers were ready for films that was more complex, real, and relatable. Pixar delivered.

I believe a similar phenomenon has occurred with many aspects of Christian theology these days—at least in the West. Pop culture has greatly confused the facts presented in Scripture. People today hold to concepts of heaven and hell that are derived from bits and pieces of the Bible as well as from medieval European folklore, Greco-Roman art and literature, Eastern influences, and Hollywood films. People's perceptions of God, the Bible, and Christianity have become a mixed bag of disjointed and competing concepts that lead to great confusion.

In art, heaven is often depicted as a place where plump babies sit on clouds and play harps. Hell is viewed as a fiery and unpleasant place run by the devil, or as a run-down underworld nightclub of sorts—where revelers get to fellowship with likeminded Hades-dwellers for eternity while wearing ragged clothes. The idea of a literal heaven and hell is often mocked, caricatured, ridiculed, or ignored—and seen as a pre-enlightenment scare tactic for controlling people's behavior.

Even in Christian circles, many have grown up with a cultural view of heaven and hell. We're not quite as confused as the culture itself, and we understand the basics on a surface level, but we still have some common misperceptions

mixed in with our understanding of biblical truth. This seems to be true about any complex area of Bible study, including the basic theology of the afterlife.

In today's church, there are certain aspects of heaven and hell that have remained overly simplified or dumbed down because we assume people can't handle the details. I believe they can. I believe when we dig into the weeds with diligence and care, the more complex truths about heaven and hell can be understood. That is what we are going to study in this chapter. I pray that you will walk away with a greater comprehension of and appreciation for heaven and hell, their purposes, their necessity, and their direct relationship to spiritual warfare.

Progressive Revelation of the Afterlife

Over the course of time as the Bible was being written, God revealed more and more information about all things, including the afterlife. In systematic theology, this is known as progressive revelation. The Old Testament understanding of the afterlife was summed up in the Hebrew word *Sheol*. This was a broad term that could refer to the unseen realm of the dead (Genesis 37:35), the actual grave where someone was buried (Psalm 141:7), a place of punishment (Psalm 55:15; Isaiah 5:14; Hosea 13:14), or a holding area for the Old Testament righteous after they died (Psalms 49:15; 86:13). Context is key in determining which of these is being indicated.

In the New Testament, the Greek word for this holding place of the dead is *Hades*. Sheol, or Hades, is always depicted as being downward, under the earth's crust, under mountains, in the lower regions of the earth, yet in the unseen realm. The parallel realities mysteriously

coexist. Sheol generally has negative, punitive connotations, with one exception, which we'll highlight below.

Most often the term (along with several others, such as the New Testament term *Gehenna*) is translated as "hell." This can be confusing because the Old Testament speaks of the righteous dead going down to *Sheol* (usually translated as "the grave").

QUICK FACT: DID YOU KNOW...

Gehenna is another name for hell that is used in the New Testament, but it is more of a word picture that used the Valley of Gehenna (just south of Jerusalem) as an example of what hell is like? It was a ritually unclean area where trash burned continually. Hell is pictured as the city dump of eternity.

But aren't the righteous supposed to go to heaven when they die? This has caused confusion for many and led to some faulty theology—most notably with regard to the concepts of soul sleep and purgatory. Soul sleep refers to the idea that, when believers die, their souls sleep until after judgment day. Then they will wake up in heaven. Those who teach the concept of purgatory say that while Jesus's sacrifice paid for some of our sins—our basic sin nature, so to speak—we still must spend some time in hell to pay for others of our sins before we can be ushered into heaven. That is, purgatory is said to purify us before we enter heaven. Both of these concepts are unbiblical and go against the clear teaching of Scripture.

1 Peter 3:18—Christ also suffered once for sins, the righteous for the unrighteous, to bring you to God. He was put to death in the body but made alive in the Spirit.

2 Corinthians 5:6-8
We are always confident and know that as long as we are at home in the body we are away from the Lord. For we live by faith, not by sight. We are confident, I say, and would prefer to be away from the body and at home with the Lord.

Once we get to the New Testament, we discover additional information that helps clear up the confusion. The basic gist of it is this: In the Old Testament era, God's people looked forward to the promise of a Savior because Jesus had not yet come. Though they were right with God through faith in a future Savior, legally speaking, their sins were not yet paid for. The prophesied transaction was as good as done but had not actually occurred yet. So the righteous dead remained in a heavenly holding place until the time that the promise was fulfilled. They went to a section of Sheol/Hades known as Paradise or Abraham's side (or bosom, in some Bible translations). The word translated "side" in Luke 16:22 is the Greek word *kólpos*.

There is no English equivalent to the word, so it is difficult to translate. The *kólpos* was an overhanging fold of the outer garments worn in that day, which formed a small pocket area near the chest. The *kólpos* is essentially a special area that is synonymous with intimacy, union, comfort, and protection. It has connotations of a baby being swaddled, or a toddler sitting on their father's lap. This special position of comfort and blessing is the general meaning of Abraham's side.

Abraham was the father of promise. God's people and the Savior of the world came from Abraham. The whole earth has indeed been blessed through Abraham's descendants (Genesis 22:18). Prior to the cross, all the righteous dead went to this comforting and blessed holding place of promise. We read about this in Luke 16. There, Jesus sheds tremendous light on the subject. It is important to note that this was not a parable but is described as an actual account. Here is what Jesus said:

ABRAHAM

> There was a rich man who was dressed in purple and fine linen and lived in luxury every day. At his gate was laid a beggar named Lazarus, covered with sores and longing to eat what fell from the rich man's table. Even the dogs came and licked his sores.
>   The time came when the beggar died and the angels carried him to Abraham's side. The rich man also died and was buried. In Hades, where he was in torment, he looked up and saw Abraham far away, with Lazarus by his side. So he called to him, "Father Abraham, have pity on me and send Lazarus to dip

the tip of his finger in water and cool my tongue, because I am in agony in this fire."

But Abraham replied, "Son, remember that in your lifetime you received your good things, while Lazarus received bad things, but now he is comforted here and you are in agony. And besides all this, between us and you a great chasm has been set in place, so that those who want to go from here to you cannot, nor can anyone cross over from there to us" (verses 19-26).

When Lazarus died, angels escorted him to Paradise (Abraham's side). When the man who was not right with God died, he went to a lower section of Hades/Sheol. This is what we would refer to as hell. It is characterized by torment, agony, fire, loneliness, and an awareness of the blessings experienced by the righteous dead. Especially noteworthy is the fact that Lazarus and the rich man ended up in fixed locations, and there is a great chasm or gulf between the place of blessing and the place of torment.

The Prison Under the Prison

There's one more component to the concept of Sheol/Hades we need to consider before we get to the fun stuff. In Scripture, we learn about another place of punishment—a dark holding cell for certain fallen angels, called *Tartarus*.

If you'll recall from our study of Genesis 6, certain fallen angels crossed a major line and procreated with human women. The flood destroyed the violent and evil offspring, and the angels who were involved in that transgression were imprisoned in a deep prison in Sheol to await final judgment.

In Jude 6 we read about those angels from Genesis 6: "The angels who did not keep their positions of authority but abandoned their proper dwelling—these he has kept in darkness, bound with everlasting chains for judgment on the great Day." And in 2 Peter 2:4, we read this: "God did not spare angels when they sinned, but sent them to hell, putting them in chains of darkness to be held for judgment." There, the word translated "hell" is the Greek term *Tartarus*. Strong's Exhaustive Concordance defines Tartarus as "the deepest abyss of Hades."

At a specific point in the future, these angels will be permanently punished in the lake of fire (more on that later). But apparently in God's lawful economy, their unlawful behavior required time in a dark dungeon first. The angels who rebelled in Genesis 6 have been doing time ever since. One day, their time on death row will be over and they will be cast into eternal fire.

The Bottomless Pit

There is one more mysterious area of the afterlife "holding pen" that Scripture mentions. The Greek term for it is *abussou*, which is translated "the Abyss," or the bottomless pit. The word is used nine times, all in the New Testament. It is where demons go when they are cast out of people (see, for example, Luke 8:31). It is also where one of the end-times judgments of Revelation will originate from when some demonic creatures are released upon the earth (Revelation 9:1-2; 11), as well as the place where Satan will be bound for 1,000 years during the millennial kingdom (Revelation 20:1-3,7-10). It appears that this is yet another section of Sheol or Hades that has a specific purpose. Most

theology diagrams depict this area as being underneath the great chasm (or one and the same) spoken of in Luke 16, which we will look at in a moment. Some theologians say that Tartarus and the Abyss are the same place, while others differentiate the two.

Degrees of Blessing and Punishment

Rewards in Heaven Via the Béma Seat

While our ticket to heaven has already been paid for by Jesus on the cross, there is still a great incentive for us to dedicate our lives to doing his work while we await his return or our death. Scripture clearly teaches there are degrees of eternal reward that will be given at what is known as the judgment seat of Christ—or (in Greek) the *béma* seat. In ancient times, the *béma* was a platform on which athletes were crowned after a competition. We read about the platform in 2 Corinthians 5:10: "We must all appear before the judgment seat of Christ, so that each of us may receive what is due us for the things done while in the body, whether good or bad."

We learn more of the details about this event in 1 Corinthians 3:11-15, where Paul wrote,

No one can lay any foundation other than the one already laid, which is Jesus Christ. If anyone builds on this foundation using gold, silver, costly stones, wood, hay or straw, their work will be shown for what it is, because the Day will bring it to light. It will be revealed with fire, and the fire will test the quality of each person's work. If what has been built survives, the builder will receive a reward. If it is burned up, the builder will suffer loss but yet will be saved—even though only as one escaping through the flames.

Among the rewards given on this occasion are what Scripture refers to as crowns. Whether these are literal crowns or they represent certain levels of responsibility and oversight, or both, I'm not sure—but there are at least five crown rewards mentioned in the Bible. We will also likely be given various opportunities to rule with Christ in the millennial kingdom (Revelation 20:4-6) based on the work we accomplish while here on earth (see Matthew 25:14-30).

INCORRUPTIBLE CROWN
1 Corinthians 9:25-27

CROWN OF LIFE
Revelation 2:10

CROWN OF GLORY
1 Peter 5:2-4

CROWN OF RIGHTEOUSNESS
2 Timothy 4:8

CROWN OF REJOICING
1 Thessalonians 2:19-20

Levels of Punishment in Hell

Just as there will be degrees of reward in heaven, there will be degrees of punishment in hell. Luke 12:42-48 describes varying degrees of punishment symbolized by either many or few lashes. To be blunt, Hitler will suffer far worse than the average lost soul in hell.

FOR FURTHER STUDY...
on the topic of degrees of punishment, see
John 19:11-12; Hebrews 10:28-29; 2 Peter 2:20-22

Notice the last four words in Revelation 20:12-13: "I saw the dead, the great and the small, standing before the throne, and books were opened; and another book was opened, which is the book of life; and the dead were judged from the things which were written in the books, according to their deeds" (NASB).

According to their deeds. When it comes to eternal punishment, we can be certain that God is 100 percent fair in his dealings. As you'll recall from earlier chapters, Scripture frequently uses legal terms to describe matters related to salvation, redemption, and punishment. The same is true about the afterlife. Someone has to pay for our sins because we can't get right with God on

our own. Jesus paid the penalty and offers us the most amazing gift ever given. It is free to us, but it cost him everything.

If we reject his offer to pay our sin debt, then we are 100 percent fairly judged based on our specific actions while we lived. Unfortunately, if we want separation from Christ in this life, he has no choice but to answer that prayer in the afterlife. Ultimately, the definition of hell is complete separation from God.

How Does All This Relate to Spiritual Warfare?

Here's how: When you know what the enemy knows, you have an advantage. You are not prone to deception. You also have hope in the promised future with all its wonder and majesty. God's promises are sure, and so is the future of those who are in Christ. That encouragement and knowledge protects you and me from the schemes and deceptions of the enemy.

We should also receive great comfort from knowing that one day God will set everything straight. Literally every evil act will be punished and every truly good act will be rewarded. Understanding there are degrees of reward in heaven should help us recognize the importance of focusing on eternal matters and desire to finish strong. Understanding there are degrees of punishment in hell should encourage us with the knowledge that God is not capricious in His judgment, but is—by his nature—fair, righteous, all-wise, and perfectly just. God's hand is on the wheel, and he knows what he is doing. We can truly rest in Him!

CHAPTER 8

Jesus's Authority over Darkness

Having disarmed the powers and authorities, he made a public spectacle of them, triumphing over them by the cross.

COLOSSIANS 2:15

Mauricio was one of the very few people well off by Brazilian standards. He lived on the outskirts of Belo Horizonte—the capital city of the state of Minas Gerais. He had a heart for people—and especially for the gospel. Each day, Mauricio or someone from his restaurant would take 40 to 60 meals to the children who lived near the city dump. The children's daily routine of digging through trash to search for food broke his heart. Our short-term mission team witnessed this unimaginable scene. Children and teenagers who lived near the dump chased city trash trucks upon arrival—as if the vehicles were delivering ice cream. These were the children Mauricio served by delivering hot meals and the gospel.

Not all the children living in those terrible conditions were friendly. Some—particularly a few of the teenagers who grew up on the street— were disrespectful or even violent at times. One such teenager—whom Mauricio had ministered to for more than a year—was infamous for his frightening behavior. Early on our trip, Mauricio had told us about this teen who was full of anger, rage, disrespect, and violent tendencies. He rejected the gospel and often heckled mission groups that came to help Mauricio. We were warned that this young man might show up—and sure enough, he did.

As our group gathered to pray on a street corner, this young man emerged— circling our group in curiosity. I didn't understand the Portuguese phrases he mumbled as he walked around us, but I'm sure they weren't good. I distinctly remember the look on his face and the intimidating posture he carried. All I can say is that it felt demonic. Others in our group agreed.

There are a surprising number of occult religions in Brazil, and missionaries often report seeing demonic activity in the course of their work. Nothing further happened that day, but Mauricio challenged us to continue praying for this young man, so we did—all week long. Then after several days, it happened.

One evening toward the end of the week, Mauricio shared some amazing news. Earlier in the day, he had a clear opportunity to present the gospel to this hostile young man once again. It seemed the Lord had used our prayers and positioned the possibly demonically influenced teen to be receptive to the message of the gospel, and he accepted Christ as his Savior.

This exciting news was great to hear but didn't really hit home until we saw the young man the next day. He was a different person—the transformation was like that of going from night to day. He was calm, smiling, joyful, and stationary instead of pacing around our group and invading people's personal space. There was a new warmth about him. This reminded me of the wild and violent man in Luke 8 who was possessed by demons and lived among the graves. After Jesus compassionately delivered the man from the demons, the people who knew him showed up and "found the man from whom the demons had gone out, sitting at Jesus' feet, dressed and in his right mind" (verse 35). The scene in Brazil felt somewhat the same.

Mauricio put his arm around the young man as he was speaking to our group and said, "This young man once was lost, but now is found. He was the possession of the enemy, but now he is the Lord's adopted child. He is a new creation in Christ!" With tearful eyes we all rejoiced and prayed that God would bless this young man and use him for the kingdom. Some hugged him. Some shook his hand with a smile. He was now a new brother in Christ; he was now free.

Jesus has authority over darkness. The battle between him and Satan is not a battle of equals. When Jesus comes in, evil must leave. There's not a demon behind every bush, but evil is more active in the lives of unbelievers than most people realize. Whether by subtle influence, oppressive tactics, or outright possession, demonic activity is occurring all around us today. Think about that for a moment. The same demons at work in the pages of Scripture are active today, trying to keep people from receiving Christ. In the words of John 10:10, the goal of the enemy is simply to "steal and kill and destroy." But the second half of that verse gives the antidote. There, Jesus says, "I have come that they may have life, and have it to the full."

The Testimony of Demons

Once Jesus began his earthly ministry after his baptism, temptation in the wilderness, and choosing the dirty dozen (his original 12 disciples), we notice a curious fact as we read through the Gospel accounts. Jesus frequently encountered people who were possessed by demons. At that time and in that area, demon possession was very prevalent. The concentrated amount of spiritual warfare demonstrates that—as we discussed in an earlier chapter—the enemy knew the time frame and region where the Messiah was to come.

26 OF THE 109 MESSIANIC PROPHECIES

PROPHECY	PREDICTION	FULFILLMENT
Isaiah 7:14	born of a virgin	Luke 1:26-53
Micah 5:2	born in Bethlehem	Matthew 2:1
Hosea 11:1	flight into Egypt	Matthew 2:14
Jeremiah 31:15	to escape death	Matthew 2:16
Genesis 49:10	from the tribe of Judah	Luke 3:33
Isaiah 7:14	called Immanuel	Matthew 1:23
Isaiah 9:1-2	ministry in Galilee	Matthew 4:12-16
Zechariah 9:9	triumphal entry into Jerusalem	Matthew 21:1-11
Psalm 41:9	betrayed by a friend	Matthew 26:20-25
Zechariah 11:12	for 30 pieces of silver	Matthew 26:15
Zechariah 11:13	money used for potter's field	Matthew 26:6-7
Isaiah 53:3	rejected by Jews	John 1:11
Psalm 35:11	falsely accused	Matthew 26:59-68
Isaiah 53:7	silent before accusers	Matthew 27:12-14
Isaiah 50:6	hit and spit on	Mark 14:65
Isaiah 53:4-5	suffered for others (us)	Matthew 8:16-17
Isaiah 53:12	crucified with robbers	Matthew 27:38
Psalm 22:16	hands and feet pierced	John 20:25
Psalm 34:20	bones not broken	John 19:33
Psalm 22:18	lots cast for garment	John 19:23-24
Psalm 22:15	thirsted on the cross	John 19:28
Psalm 69:21	and given vinegar	John 19:29
Psalm 22:1	"My God, why did you forsake me?"	Matthew 27:46
Isaiah 53:9	buried in tomb of rich	Matthew 27:57-61
Psalm 16:10	resurrection	Matthew 28:9
Psalm 68:18	ascension	Luke 24:50-51

When Jesus encountered these demons, they knew who he was. Mark and Luke both record an event in Capernaum where Jesus cast a demon out of a man in a synagogue. As Jesus taught in the synagogue, people were amazed at his teaching and authority. This apparently upset the demon in a man who was in attendance. Mark 1:23-26 says,

> Just then a man in their synagogue who was possessed by an impure spirit cried out, "What do you want with us, Jesus of Nazareth? Have you come to destroy us? I know who you are—the Holy One of God!" "Be quiet!" said Jesus sternly. "Come out of him!" The impure spirit shook the man violently and came out of him with a shriek.

There are several facts to note from this passage. First, there was a demon in church, and nobody realized it. Second, when God's Word is proclaimed with authority, there will be resistance. Third, demons know exactly who Jesus is. Fourth, demons know Bible prophecy and that there is an appointed time of judgment coming. Fifth, Jesus has authority over all—even the powerful fallen beings who have rebelled against God himself.

After the demon was cast out, we read that "the people were all so amazed that they asked each other, 'What is this? A new teaching—and with authority! He even gives orders to impure spirits and they obey him'" (Mark 1:27). For them, this was a new development, and it coincided with Jesus's earlier proclamation that "the time has come" and "the kingdom of God has come near" (verse 15). Though his future physical kingdom would not come until after the end of the church age, Jesus embodied the kingdom of God. The authority and wisdom of this teacher caught everyone by surprise—human and demonic alike.

We find another key account of Jesus asserting his authority over demons in Mark 5 and Luke 8. After asserting his authority over the weather and calming an intense, curiously timed storm, Jesus and his disciples made it to shore and were immediately met by a demon-possessed man.

Let's read the full account of what happened in Luke 8:27-39:

> When Jesus stepped ashore, he was met by a demon-possessed man from the town. For a long time this man had not worn clothes or lived

in a house, but had lived in the tombs. When he saw Jesus, he cried out and fell at his feet, shouting at the top of his voice, *"What do you want with me, Jesus, Son of the Most High God? I beg you, don't torture me!"* For Jesus had commanded the impure spirit to come out of the man. Many times it had seized him, and though he was chained hand and foot and kept under guard, he had broken his chains and had been driven by the demon into solitary places.

Jesus asked him, "What is your name?" "Legion," he replied, because many demons had gone into him. *And they begged Jesus repeatedly not to order them to go into the Abyss.* A large herd of pigs was feeding there on the hillside. The demons begged Jesus to let them go into the pigs, and he gave them permission. When the demons came out of the man, they went into the pigs, and the herd rushed down the steep bank into the lake and was drowned.

When those tending the pigs saw what had happened, they ran off and reported this in the town and countryside, and the people went out to see what had happened. When they came to Jesus, *they found the man from whom the demons had gone out, sitting at Jesus' feet, dressed and in his right mind*; and they were afraid. Those who had seen it told the people how the demon-possessed man had been cured.

Then all the people of the region of the Gerasenes asked Jesus to leave them, because they were overcome with fear. So he got into the boat and left. The man from whom the demons had gone out begged to go with him, but Jesus sent him away, saying, "Return home and tell how much God has done for you." So the man went away and told all over town how much Jesus had done for him (emphasis added).

Once again, we discover that the demons knew who Jesus was—the son of the Most High God. They also knew that judgment was coming for them at some point, and that they had no choice but to obey the authoritative command of

Jesus. In this account, we learn a couple more things about demons: namely, that several of them can inhabit one person, and that it is possible for demons to possess animals. Based on this biblical evidence, I believe that some split personality disorders are cases of demon possession, and I believe that some violent animal attacks upon humans may possibly be demonically influenced.

The demons in Luke 8 wanted to avoid going to the Abyss. They wanted to continue their free reign for as long as possible. Like out-of-control gang members, they were consumed with committing evil every chance they had. Their request of Jesus to cast them into pigs instead of the Abyss was granted. I don't know why, but I do trust Jesus had a purpose for allowing that. Though the demons avoided the immediate punishment of being cast into the Abyss, they won't avoid final judgment when they are cast into the lake of fire along with all of the other evil entities.

Some Bible commentaries say the pigs went insane when the demons entered them, and that is why they ran off the cliff. This is speculation, but I think it is more likely that the evil spirits intentionally caused the pigs to plummet to their death so they could be free to search for another human host (see Matthew 12:43-45).

Matthew 12:43-45—When an impure spirit comes out of a person, it goes through arid places seeking rest and does not find it. Then it says, "I will return to the house I left." When it arrives, it finds the house unoccupied, swept clean and put in order. Then it goes and takes with it seven other spirits more wicked than itself, and they go in and live there. And the final condition of that person is worse than the first.

As we read this account and others like it, we cannot help but notice the great compassion Jesus had for people. Despite the man's frightening appearance, Jesus spoke directly to him with a simple question: "What is your name?" Then after the ordeal we find the man sitting at Jesus's feet fully clothed. Assuming there wasn't a nearby Walmart, this means Jesus and the disciples provided him with clothes. They restored his dignity along with his sanity. The before-and-after description of the man reminds me of the story I shared at the opening of this chapter. The difference in him was as clear as that between night and day. This is the kind of life-change Jesus can bring—even to those who have been trapped for a very long time.

Before the cross, Jesus often kept demons from speaking and spilling the beans about his identity (see Mark 1:34; Luke 4:41). I think this had to do with more than the Savior rejecting the testimony of filthy demons because Jesus also told some people not to tell others who he was (Mark 1:44-45) and that his time had not yet come (John 2:4; 7:6). But after the cross, he announced his identity with a bullhorn.

Three Mysterious Days

Have you ever wondered why there were three days between Jesus's death and his resurrection? One reason is because that made it very obvious that he truly was dead and that the resurrection was for real. The three-day interval also fulfilled Bible prophecy. But consider this as well: Where was Jesus's spirit during those three days? Was he just sitting next to his body looking at his watch until three days had gone by?

Before dying on the cross, Jesus told us where he would go during the time between his death and resurrection. In Matthew 12:38-42, we read,

> Some of the Pharisees and teachers of the law said to him, "Teacher, we want to see a sign from you." He answered, "A wicked and adulterous generation asks for a sign! But none will be given it except the sign of the prophet Jonah. For as Jonah was three days and three nights in the belly of a huge fish, so the Son of Man will be three days and three nights in the heart of the earth."

Some theologians believe that during those three days, Jesus went to Sheol/Hades. They point to 1 Peter 3:18-20, which says,

Christ also suffered once for sins, the righteous for the unrighteous, to bring you to God. He was put to death in the body but made alive in the Spirit. After being made alive, he went and made proclamation to the imprisoned spirits—to those who were disobedient long ago when God waited patiently in the days of Noah while the ark was being built. In it only a few people, eight in all, were saved through water.

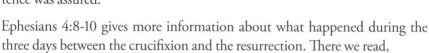

Some Bible scholars take this to mean that Jesus went to show the angels imprisoned in Tartarus (which we read about in the previous chapter) that He had accomplished his mission to pay for the sins of mankind. Essentially, he was letting them know that their fate was sealed. Their future permanent death sentence was assured.

Ephesians 4:8-10 gives more information about what happened during the three days between the crucifixion and the resurrection. There we read,

> When he ascended on high, he took many captives and gave gifts to his people. (What does "he ascended" mean except that he also descended to the lower, earthly regions? He who descended is the very one who ascended higher than all the heavens, in order to fill the whole universe.)

In modern English, that passage is saying that during the three days between Jesus's death and resurrection, Christ took the righteous dead from paradise into heaven, where God dwells, and gave them gifts. The gifts may have been similar to the eternal rewards church-age believers will be given at the *béma* seat of Christ. They may also have been given their living quarters in heaven, similar to what church-age believers will receive after the rapture.

John 14:3—If I go and prepare a place for you, I will come back and take you to be with me that you also may be where I am.

If you'll recall, when Jesus hung on the cross, one of the criminals believed in him. and Jesus told the man, "Truly I tell you, today you will be with me in paradise" (Luke 23:43). In other words, Jesus was highlighting the fact that both he and the believing criminal were about to die—but afterward they would both be comforted at Abraham's side, the place of Paradise.

The promise had been kept. The prophecies of the Messiah and his atoning death had been fulfilled. This was a game changer on many levels—not the least of which was the location of the righteous believers who had died prior to the time of the cross. The cross set the final-phase wheels in motion. Because of that single event, paradise changed zip codes and moved to heaven, where God dwells. And it is only a matter of time until Jesus comes to rapture the church, judge the world, and relocate hell's zip code to the lake of fire.

My Dad Is Bigger Than Your Dad

I'm a child of the 1970s, and I don't know if kids still compare their dads, but way back then (easy, now—I'm not *that* old yet!), I remember when kids, in a game of one-upmanship, would say, "My dad is bigger than your dad. My dad can beat your dad. He can run faster than your dad."

As we consider the power that Jesus had over demons during his earthly ministry and his epic conquest of death via the cross and the resurrection, we can take confidence in his authority over all things. Jesus was given this authority by the Father. As Matthew 28:18 says, "all authority in heaven and on earth" have been given to Jesus.

When we understand that Jesus performed a proverbial touchdown celebration before the imprisoned fallen angels in Tartarus, we rejoice. When we learn about how he comforted the righteous Old Testament saints and organized their cross-cosmos relocation, we celebrate. When we understand that God has a 100 percent track record of fulfilling prophecy, we stand confident in our future. We know that the enemy is as good as dead. It's just a matter of time before the remaining prophecies prove true and come to pass. In all of this we can take great joy, for those of us who belong to Christ can know with absolute certainty that for all eternity, we will stand as victors in this war that has consumed all of human history.

CHAPTER 9

The Believer's Authority over Darkness

You are of God, little children,
and have overcome them,
because He who is in you is greater
than he who is in the world.

1 JOHN 4:4 (NKJV)

As we rounded the bend in the batey (pronounced bah-tey), we saw what looked like a strange, primitive military fort. Large, thick branches had been meticulously stuck into the ground every two inches apart. The odd makeshift fence completely surrounded a small house made of a patchwork of tin roofing scraps and wooden planks. Amidst the scores of other shanties in the batey, this one was obviously different, and we would soon find out why.

ba•tey = A (usually very impoverished) settlement based around a
noun sugar mill.

As we approached the house, the missionaries we were serving with gathered us for a huddle. They gave us the rundown on the house and why we had stopped there. This was the house of the local voodoo priest. He had established himself as the religious leader of the batey and constantly undermined the missionaries' work there.

In the Dominican Republic, the bateyes are near the Haitian border and house second- and third-generation Haitians who are, for the most part, stuck there. Most have few family roots in Haiti (which is poorer than the D.R.), and very little chance of ever integrating into Dominican society. They have no running water, no sewage system, no hospitals, no education, and no police force. Due to the lack of education and outside influence, the Haitian roots of voodoo die hard in many of the bateyes.

The missionaries had brought the gospel, basic hygiene, education, and a medical clinic to this particular batey, but found themselves in a constant tug-of-war with the voodoo belief system engrained in the local culture. So they decided to bring out the big guns—the prayers of God's people. Our group of about 30 people spread out and held hands—encircling as much of the small compound as we could—and we prayed against the evil that had established itself there. We prayed for the salvation of the voodoo priest and the people in the batey, and we prayed against the evil forces in the unseen realm. Satan had a stronghold here, and we wanted to see it broken.

A short time after our team returned from the trip, we received some news from the missionaries. The voodoo priest's house had completely burned down. They didn't know how or why, but it happened. The voodoo priest doubled down, however, and set up shop in a smaller shanty in the batey. After the fire, he seemed to come against the work of the missionaries even more aggressively. Then another short-term mission team served in that batey. They did the same thing we had done—they prayed that God would eradicate the evil stronghold there.

The next time we talked with the missionaries, they shared some interesting news. The youngish voodoo priest—who was in his thirties—suddenly dropped dead one day. That is not what we had prayed for, but apparently it was God's planned outcome. We had prayed for his salvation. Perhaps when his house had burned down, that was his chance for redemption. The bottom line is that we prayed that the dark, demonic stronghold in this batey would be broken, and—by the power of the cross and in the name of Jesus—it was!

The Difference Between Might and Authority

Mills Lane is in the boxing hall of fame. Not so much for boxing (though he did have a boxing career during the 1960s), but for refereeing. He officiated several heavyweight championship boxing matches from the 1970s through the 1990s—refereeing boxers who were up to 100 pounds heavier, a foot-and-a-half taller, and a quarter-century younger than him. Despite these notable differences, Mills Lane controlled the bouts with impeccable prowess, professionalism, and authority.

Any of the heavyweights could have knocked Mills Lane clear out of the ring, but the seasoned referee had one thing on his side—the full weight and authority of the boxing governing board. As believers, you and I have a similar arrangement. Though we face powerful evil entities much stronger than we are, we have the full weight of Christ's authority within us.

Though Satan and his fallen horde are vastly more powerful than humans, they have no power over believers. The authority we have through our relationship with Christ overrides any power the enemy might try to leverage against us. He can lie and tempt in an effort to limit our effectiveness, but he is restrained from doing anything to us that is not filtered through the loving hands of an omnipotent and omniscient God. The enemy may throw a lot at us. He can harass and oppress at times, to be sure—especially when we are fully submitted to the Lord and engaged in effective ministry. The enemy will attempt to use our fleshly nature and the sinful world system against us. But the more we walk in the light of God's truth and apply it to our lives, the less effective the enemy's tactics become. The bottom line is that we, by virtue of God's power, have authority over the darkness.

Satan and his network of evil will use every tactic they can to tempt us to shrink back. He wants us to give up and give in. He wants to minimize our effectiveness by tempting us with sin and weakening our resolve. He tells us lies. Like a schoolyard bully, he threatens us that if we stand up he will punch us even harder. But the power of the bully is taken away by our stand—and the omnipotent God who stands behind us. The beauty of it is we don't stand in our own strength but in the power and authority of Christ, who defeated the enemy at the cross and "made a public spectacle" of him (Colossians 2:15). So why does the enemy fight so hard against us? Why are we even in this battle to begin with?

Caught in the Middle

C.S. Lewis made this astute observation: "Enemy-occupied territory—that is what this world is. Christianity is the story of how the rightful king has landed, you might say landed in disguise, and is calling us to take part in a great campaign of sabotage."[1]

Even though we didn't sign up for it, you and I are caught in the middle of this battle whether we realize it or not. The age-old war in the unseen realm has profound effects on the world in which we live. From individual struggles with sin and addiction to international geopolitical subterfuge to covert planning by high-powered figures influenced by the occult, there is a prolific and direct war being waged all around us. We are in enemy territory.

The Christian life is not lived on a playground, but a battleground. When we tune in to the latest news on any given day, we witness the extent of the cosmic battle that affects all of us. The Bible does not pull punches about this; it warns us in clear terms. For example, in 1 Peter 5:8 we read, "Be alert and of sober mind. Your enemy the devil prowls around like a roaring lion looking for someone to devour." The worst thing we can do is to ignore the raging war or deny its reality. That would be like standing in a boxing ring with your hands down and your back to your opponent. Mills Lane, even with all his authority, can't help you there. We need to protect ourselves at all times. We need to stand strong!

When you peel back the layers of world history and conflict you will find a deeper evil lurking in the darkest of places. The Nazis, for example, were not just a twisted political group—they were steeped in the occult at the highest levels of their ranks. Radical Islam is not just an aberrant off-shoot of Islam; it engages in activities designed to steal, kill, and destroy (see John 10:10).

The battle all around us is very real, but the good news is that Satan and God are not equal opposites. God is omniscient, omnipresent, and omnipotent. That means he knows all, sees all (is present everywhere at once), and is all-powerful. Satan is omninothing. He can be in only one place at a time, has broad but limited knowledge, and immense but limited power. Yet in his own self-deception, he thinks he can outwit God. While Satan and his demonic horde are individually limited, together they comprise a twisted global network that attempts to mimic God's omni attributes.

While there are levels of authority and power within this present darkness, the believer—when faced with such evil—has authority over all of them. Again,

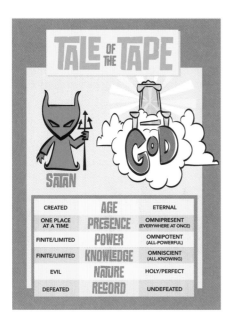

TALE OF THE TAPE

SATAN | | GOD

CREATED	**AGE**	ETERNAL
ONE PLACE AT A TIME	**PRESENCE**	OMNIPRESENT (EVERYWHERE AT ONCE)
FINITE/LIMITED	**POWER**	OMNIPOTENT (ALL-POWERFUL)
FINITE/LIMITED	**KNOWLEDGE**	OMNISCIENT (ALL-KNOWING)
EVIL	**NATURE**	HOLY/PERFECT
DEFEATED	**RECORD**	UNDEFEATED

this is *not* based on our own strength, but grounded in the power of Christ alone. We can rebuke the enemy only in the name and power of Jesus Christ. When we who know Christ as Savior claim his name, we're like Mills Lane standing in the boxing ring with an authority much bigger than our own. Though we are weak and sinful, Christ is not. As 1 John 4:4 states, the one who is in us is much greater than the one who is in the world.

Through the cross we can be forgiven. Then we stand in the power and authority of Christ. If you are a believer, you have switched sides. You have been rescued from the power of the enemy. You have gone from darkness to light (Acts 26:18). When that happened, you were marked by the enemy—yet you are also sealed and protected by the Holy Spirit! (Ephesians 1:13-14).

As believers in Christ, we are indwelt by the Holy Spirit and we are the salt and light of the earth. God uses our lives and influence to preserve the world from complete corruption. Much like the account of the missionaries in the bateyes, God desires for believers to shine brightly into dark places—exposing evil for what it is and dispelling its stranglehold wherever we bring the light of Christ.

The enemy hates losing territory. When a person is an unbeliever, he does everything possible to keep that person from coming to Christ. Once someone is saved, the enemy will do everything possible to minimize their effectiveness and testimony. Our ancient foe also wants to hurt God any way he can. Every parent knows that the worst way someone can hurt them is by hurting one of their kids. That may sound scary, but God has given us the tools to fight the battle. He has not left us to fend for ourselves.

The question, then, is not about *if* we will have spiritual battles. The question is whether we will purposefully engage in them. To do so calls for us to continually and increasingly submit to the Lord and his will for our lives. This is the best protection we have against the enemy's schemes. There is no safer place for us to be than in the center of God's will. In chapters 10–17 of this book, we'll discuss just how to do this on a practical level by putting on our spiritual armor.

This does not mean we will always be saved from harm or struggle, but we can rest assured that no harm or struggle will come our way unless it is filtered through the Father's hands and serves his purposes. God will allow the enemy to come against us only when the outcome can work for our good (Romans 8:28) and God's glory (1 Corinthians 10:31). Martin Luther is quoted as saying, "Even the devil is God's devil." Ultimately, all evil will be leveraged to achieve God's purposes.

That said, we'll also see throughout the second half of this book that we can't live in unholiness and expect to fight spiritual battles successfully. To be effective, we must be continually submitted to Christ, growing in Him and abiding in Him. As we learn the enemy's tactics and as we learn to align our thoughts, motives, and actions with the purposes of God, we gain strength for the daily battles.

MARTIN LUTHER

As Paul said in Romans 8:37, "We are more than conquerors through him who loved us." As John informs us in Revelation 12:11, believers triumph over the enemy "by the blood of the Lamb and by the word of their testimony." Through the power of Christ, we are able to stand strong through the battles and live out our testimony. We stand in victory already, but we must fight for it at the same time. We live in a paradoxical already-but-not-yet scenario.

When you encounter spiritual darkness in any form—whether subtle influences in your thinking, or clear and present demonic activity as described in some of the missionary stories I've shared—you can stand on the authority of Christ and rebuke it. This is not self-confidence, but confidence in the one to whom you belong.

Verses from the Arsenal

Throughout the remaining chapters of this book we'll discuss specifically how to fight the battle. But before we look at the spiritual armor Paul details in Ephesians chapter 6, here are a few verses you may want to keep handy to remind you of your security in Christ:

> Romans 8:31—"What then shall we say to these things? If God is for us, who can be against us?"

> 1 John 4:4—"You are of God, little children, and have overcome them, because He who is in you is greater than he who is in the world" (NKJV).

> James 4:7—"Submit to God. Resist the devil and he will flee from you" (NKJV).

> 2 Corinthians 2:14—"Now thanks be to God who always leads us in triumph in Christ, and through us diffuses the fragrance of His knowledge in every place" (NKJV).

> Colossians 1:12-13—"[Give] thanks to the Father who has qualified us to be partakers of the inheritance of the saints in the light. He has delivered us from the power of darkness and conveyed us into the kingdom of the Son of His love" (NKJV).

> 2 Corinthians 10:4-6—"The weapons we fight with are not the weapons of the world. On the contrary, they have divine power to demolish strongholds. We demolish arguments and every pretension that sets itself up against the knowledge of God, and we take captive every thought to make it obedient to Christ. And we will be ready to punish every act of disobedience, once your obedience is complete."

The Importance of Authenticity

In Acts 19, we read an interesting account about some posers. They didn't know Jesus but wanted to leverage his name. Who knows what their motivation was? Perhaps fame and recognition. Perhaps they wanted to gain a following. Or maybe they had good intentions but didn't realize the necessity of knowing Jesus as Savior. Whatever the reason, things did not turn out well for them.

They had heard the stories about Jesus and the apostles casting out demons, and though they didn't know Christ as Savior themselves, they tried to invoke his authority over the dark forces in the spiritual realm. Here's what happened:

> Some Jews who went around driving out evil spirits tried to invoke the name of the Lord Jesus over those who were demon-possessed. They would say, "In the name of the Jesus whom Paul preaches, I command you to come out." Seven sons of Sceva, a Jewish chief priest, were doing this. One day the evil spirit answered them, "Jesus I know, and Paul I know about, but who are you?" Then the man who had the evil spirit jumped on them and overpowered them all. He gave them such a beating that they ran out of the house naked and bleeding (verses 13-16).

DR. PHIL

One can be religious but not know Jesus. A person can know Scripture, go to church, talk about spiritual things, and look the part. But when it comes to spiritual things, when the rubber meets the road, you can't fake it. Only an authentic relationship with Christ will give someone victory over demonic forces.

Your Battle

What battles are you facing right now that may have a spiritual component? You may not be facing a voodoo priest or a demon-possessed person, but the enemy works in countless subtle ways in his attempt to defeat God's children.

Perhaps you have some long-term struggles you can't seem to break, some self-defeating thought patterns that have become ingrained into your mind, or some deep-seated anger over a terrible

BATTLEFIELD TACTICS

event that happened to you many years ago. Or perhaps you—like the sons of Sceva—do not yet know the Lord. I bring up that last possibility because, as we study Paul's teaching about the believer's spiritual armor, it is vitally important that you know Christ as Savior first. No armor will be effective if you don't know the Armor Maker.

If you don't know Jesus as your personal Savior, today would be a great day to put your trust in him. Pause here and go to the last chapter of the book to read the ABCs of salvation. Then turn your attention back to here so you can learn from Paul's instructions in Ephesians chapter 6.

Now that you're all set, let's turn the page and get ready to suit up!

SECTION 3:

SUITING UP FOR BATTLE

CHAPTER 10

Ephesians 6

The weapons we fight with are not the weapons of the world. On the contrary, they have divine power to demolish strongholds. We demolish arguments and every pretension that sets itself up against the knowledge of God, and we take captive every thought to make it obedient to Christ.

2 CORINTHIANS 10:4-5

The Roman war machine was known for its efficiency, swiftness, organization, and merciless execution. At the heart of the Roman military—and the growth and stability of the Roman Empire—was the Roman soldier, the most elite warrior of his time. Modern-day military colleges still study the tactics and training of ancient Rome's fighting forces.

As part of his preparation, the Roman soldier had to complete an 18.4-mile march with all of his equipment and rations in under five hours. He had weapons training every morning, during which he would practice with equipment much heavier than what he actually used in battle. The Roman soldier also practiced many specific drills, tactics, and formations for every battle scenario imaginable. They were the special-ops forces of the day. Fighting and war was all they knew.

Key to the soldier's success in battle was his armor—both offensive and defensive equipment. Each piece was meticulously designed and refined for a specific purpose. Each had been battle-tested and refined to serve well. Each was critical to the success and survival of the Roman solder during battle. And each was so thoroughly ingrained in the soldier's training that it would essentially become an extension of the soldier.

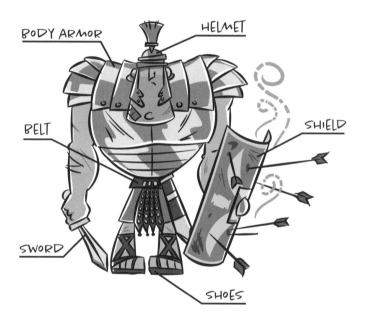

There were 28 legions (at the time of the Jewish historian Josephus in the first century AD) of roughly 6,000 men in the Roman army. That is a fighting force of almost 170,000 soldiers. Each legion had a unique name and number. Each also had its own fortress. In modern military terms, there were 28 Roman military bases spread throughout the Roman Empire.[1]

There were two main types of solders: legionaries and auxiliaries. Legionaries were Roman citizens. The auxiliaries were the main fighting force and were not Roman citizens. Auxiliaries could earn full Roman citizenship for themselves and their descendants (along with a pension and some land) after a lifetime of service (25 years).[2] Soldiers could also earn various gifts and rewards for bravery in battle. Though it was called the Roman army, most solders came from other areas as the Empire grew. The army had soldiers from Africa, France, Germany, Spain, and even from the Middle East.[3]

Just as the Roman soldier was part of the whole army but stationed in a specific legion with a unique number and name, so does every believer have his or her assigned role. God has specifically placed you in this generation in an appointed area with a specific background for His ordained purpose. Nothing about your life is random. God is sovereign over all. He put you together in your mother's womb and meticulously planned every day of your life (Psalm 139:13-16).

Keep in mind that the auxiliary soldiers had to earn their citizenship, retirement plan, and land ownership. We, on the other hand, have been made citizens of heaven through faith in the Son of God, who earned that privilege for us through his death on the cross.

His resurrection was our victory, and through it we have an eternal retirement plan and a place in heaven. We sign up for a lifetime of service out of thankfulness for what God has already done.

In addition to these spectacular gifts, we also have the opportunity to earn eternal rewards. Just as Roman soldiers were given special rewards for extreme bravery in battle, we too will be awarded at the *béma* seat of Christ based on how we made use of the time and opportunities we were given.

Critical Context

Before we begin our study of Ephesians 6, we need to examine some contextual information about the book of Ephesians. For a correct understanding of Scripture, context is key. The book of Ephesians was written by Paul around AD 60–61 and is one of the four letters he wrote while imprisoned in Rome. The other three prison epistles are Philippians, Colossians, and Philemon.

Ephesians is one of Paul's most formal letters, and it deals with some core Christian principles. As a Roman citizen in a Roman prison guarded by Roman soldiers, Paul would have been very familiar with Roman soldiers and their armor.

The letter is divided into two sections. Chapters 1–3 highlight key theological truths about salvation—namely, our position in Christ. Chapters 4–6 provide instructions on how our position in Christ should influence the way we live. Our position in heaven should affect our actions on earth. The key themes of Paul's letter to the Ephesians conclude with his instructions about spiritual warfare and how to contend with it by making use of the full armor of God.

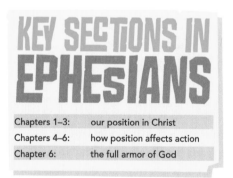

KEY SECTIONS IN EPHESIANS

Chapters 1–3:	our position in Christ
Chapters 4–6:	how position affects action
Chapter 6:	the full armor of God

The logic of the letter flows like this: Here's the theology behind our faith; here's the behavior that should result from it; and here's the battle gear you'll need to live it out successfully. It is as if Paul was saying, "You're saved now. This is a big deal. Because you are right with God, let your life show it. And, by the way, you're also in the middle of a cosmic war now—so here's your battle equipment. You're gonna need it to pull this off."

Critical Observations

With that overview of Ephesians in mind, let's take a closer look at Paul's setup for the seven pieces of armor we are told to put on. As your read these verses, consider everything we've learned so far in this book: the creation of the heavenly beings, the rebellion of the anointed cherub and one-third of the angels, the creation and fall of man, the millennia-spanning seed war prophesied in Genesis 3:15, the incursion of the mysterious Nephilim, the Babylonian backdrop, the nuances of heaven and hell and Jesus's victory over darkness, and our authority over evil forces via our standing in Christ as believers. Keep all of that running in the background of your thinking as you read these four theologically dense verses that set up Paul's teaching about our spiritual armor.

> *Be strong in the Lord and in his mighty power.* Put on the *full* armor of God, so that you can take your stand against the devil's schemes. For *our struggle is not against flesh and blood*, but against the rulers, against the authorities, against the powers of this dark world and against the spiritual forces of evil in the heavenly realms. Therefore put on the full armor of God, so that *when* the day of evil comes, you may be able to *stand your ground*, and after you have done everything, to stand (Ephesians 6:10-13, emphasis added).

There are a few key principles I'd like to point out. First, our strength is in the Lord—not our own ability, grit, determination, or toughness. We may have some natural God-given strengths and abilities, but those can feed our pride and set us up for defeat. It is vitally important that we determine to be strong in the Lord *alone*. He is our superpower and the sole source of our strength in battle.

John 15:4-5—Abide in Me, and I in you. As the branch cannot bear fruit of itself unless it abides in the vine, so neither can you unless you abide in Me. I am the vine, you are the branches; he who abides in Me and I in him, he bears much fruit, for apart from Me you can do nothing (NASB).

Second, we are told to put on the full armor of God. A soldier can't go into battle with a helmet and no sword, or shoes and no shield. Each piece is vitally important. If we allow gaps in our armor, those are the places where the enemy will focus. If we have pet sins we do not deal with, then we are going into battle with glaring weaknesses that make us vulnerable.

The enemy will always attack where we are weakest. Those are the areas we must shore up the most. Targeted Bible study, prayer, ongoing accountability, and specific steps toward our goals to overcome sin and weakness are key in this battle, which is very real. We can't play around with dynamite. Eventually it will blow up.

Third—and this has been the focus of much of this book so far—our daily battle is not against flesh and blood. It is easy for us to get caught up in human affairs, whether they be in our personal lives or as we view all that is going on around us in the world. But we must keep in mind that everything we see is being influenced by the unseen realm, and that is where the real battle exists.

There are layers and levels of evil that we contend against. Paul calls them rulers, authorities, powers of darkness, spiritual forces of evil in the heavenly realm. Different Bible translations render these categories of evil in different ways, but the bottom line is this: There is an entire intricate system of evil in this world that is warring against God's people and God's ways. This evil network touches on every aspect of world events and is much more influential than most people realize.

EPHESIANS 6:12
ARCHAS (PRINCIPALITIES)
EXOUSIAS (AUTHORITIES)
KOSMOKRATORAS (RULERS)
PNEUMATIKA (WICKED SPIRITS)

Fourth, we all face days of evil (Ephesians 6:13). Notice the passage does not say *if* the day of evil comes, but *when*. Here's the plain truth: We will all face battles in life. That is a cold, hard fact. The good news is that we don't stand alone, and God has given us the armor we need to protect ourselves as we fight.

HERE YOU GO. YOU'RE GOING TO NEED THIS.

Finally, we need to stand our ground. Four times in five verses, Paul uses the word *stand*. At the end of verse 13 he essentially says, "After you've done all this fighting, your goal is to still be on your feet. Don't get knocked out. Don't take a dive. Fight to the very end and stand!" You may struggle with a sin that has knocked you down hundreds of times. Get up and stand. You may struggle with depression or anxiety and feel like every day is a battle just to move forward. Stand. You may have faced the horrific and unexpected loss of a loved one and wondered where God is. Stand. You may be facing a life-threatening illness and it is all you can think about. Stand.

Stand and fight. If you get knocked down, get up and fight some more. The Lord promises us it will be worth it. Paul delivers these encouraging words in Romans 8:18: "I consider that our present sufferings are not worth comparing with the glory that will be revealed in us." Trials can consume us in the heat of the battle, but we must trust Scripture and take God at his word. In just a little while, we will all be standing on the shores of heaven— and it will all be worth it. Ask Job. Ask Paul. Ask John. Ask Jesus.

In the meantime, we fight. In order to survive the battles, fight with courage and dedication, and finish strong, we must spend effort and time learning the weapons of our warfare. We must train like elite soldiers at this thing called life. Most importantly, we must apply what we've learned when we are in the heat of the battle. This isn't a cakewalk, it's a war march. We aren't on a playground, but a battleground.

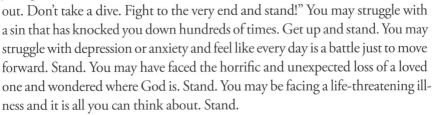

Thankfully God has given us exactly what we need to succeed. Ultimately, "the battle is not yours, but God's" (2 Chronicles 20:15). He knows we are caught in the middle and provides specific supernatural armor for us to use. As we study each piece of armor over the next seven chapters, understand that this is where the rubber meets the road. All the previous chapters in this book provide the necessary background information for the practical insights we're about to learn from Paul's powerful words in Ephesians 6. So get ready to learn about and put on your armor—one piece at a time.

CHAPTER 11

The Belt of Truth

Stand firm then, with the belt of truth buckled around your waist.

EPHESIANS 6:14

The first piece of armor Paul cites concerns the foundational elements of personal integrity and biblical truth. Our word needs to be our bond. Our commitments need to be honored. Our honesty must be core to our character. The baseline of our armor is only as strong as our honesty and integrity. This protects us from the lies and schemes of the enemy.

There is no better way to bring down a building than to destroy its foundation. Once a foundation is destroyed, the structure collapses under its own weight. On a personal level, our foundation is our integrity. In engineering terms, the word *integrity* is concerned with how stable the core structure is. That idea serves as an accurate word picture of what personal integrity is all about.

How many leaders have we seen fall due to a lack of integrity? On the surface, everything looked great, but beneath the surface—in the hidden areas that only God sees—the foundation was weak due to a lack of integrity. Eventually, the flaws in the foundation caused the whole structure to crumble.

integrity   **noun**
The quality of being honest.
Moral uprightness.
Also, the state of being whole/undivided.

The enemy is sly and multifaceted in his attack. Not only does he tempt us to compromise our personal integrity, but he also attacks biblical truth itself. The purpose of both tactics is to develop a weak spot in our spiritual armor. In the West, the enemy has been attacking biblical truth at its foundation for many years. We have been taught by the "experts" that we are mere accidents—cosmic anomalies here by complete random chance. Evolution is taught as fact. Biblical morality is under attack. Skeptics attempt to discredit the reliability of Scripture. Truth itself has been redefined as mere preference based on individual beliefs—however nonsensical. Logic is no longer widely taught in our schools, and postmodern secular humanism dominates the ideals and philosophies of Western culture.

What Is Truth?

Pontius Pilate's famous question to Jesus reverberates down through the ages (see John 18:38). Postmodern philosophies teach that truth is relative—that it is not a fixed standard, but a moving target based on the one holding to that "truth." This self-defeating philosophy could not be further *from* the truth. If someone tells you that truth is relative, just ask them if they believe that statement to be true. The foolish notion collapses under its own weight—just like a building would were it not built using the *truths* of engineering, math, and physics.

John 18:37-38—Jesus answered, "You say that I am a King. In fact, the reason I was born and came into the world is to testify to the truth. Everyone on the side of truth listens to me." "What is truth?" retorted Pilate.

Whether we know the truth about something or not is a different matter. Our perceptions may be different. If I'm color blind, I may think a red object is green, but the truth of the color itself is still there. To be sure, truth in every sphere of reality—both seen and unseen—exists. Facts matter and they are concrete, despite how dimly or well lit they are.

When it comes to the Christian faith, we can't prove that it is true in a strict scientific sense. I can't show God to an atheist. I can't take an evolutionist back in time to witness creation. I can't provide video footage of Jesus dying on the cross then exiting the tomb a few days later. If we could prove these things from a scientific standpoint, there would be no requirement for faith. God designed it this way—for faith is what demonstrates we have truly placed our trust in God.

Hebrews 11:6—Without faith it is impossible to please God, because anyone who comes to him must believe that he exists and that he rewards those who earnestly seek him.

While we can't prove these things, we can point to patterns of evidence. Like a crime scene detective, we can analyze concrete facts to determine what truth they support. Factual data either supports or disproves a given theory. I am convinced that there is an overwhelming body of evidence that supports what Scripture teaches as truth.

For example, we can use logic to show an atheist that there must have been a *first cause*—and that this first cause must be eternal. To the evolutionist we can point out the impossibility of DNA or complex molecular machines arising by mere chance.

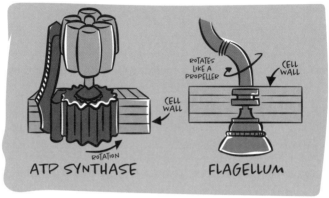

EXAMPLES OF
MOLECULAR MACHINES

ATP SYNTHASE

FLAGELLUM

To skeptics we can show the extrabiblical (outside of the Bible) accounts of non-Christian historians who recorded the events of the cross and resurrection. We can demonstrate how fulfilled Bible prophecy, archeology, and the large amount of manuscript evidence supports the accuracy and divine nature of the Bible.

QUICK FACT: DID YOU KNOW...

that over 25,000 partial and complete New Testament manuscripts have been found?[1]

While we can't *prove* those things that the Bible says are true, well-reasoned evidence coupled with faith can lead us to solid personal convictions about what is true and what is not. Our first conviction must be that truth can be known. Our next conviction as believers must be that God is trustworthy and that his Word is accurate—down to the smallest detail. A lifetime of study and walking with the Lord only strengthens this conviction for those of us who call him our Savior.

True biblical Christianity is not a blind kind of faith, but a faith based on an overwhelming amount of forensic support. I believe that all truth is God's truth.

Though we see as if we were looking in a mirror dimly (1 Corinthians 13:12 NASB), we see enough truth to put our faith in the One who claimed to be *the* Truth (John 14:6).

The Bible is under attack because the enemy knows that if he can gut the truth, then he's taken out the foundation of our armor. God's truth was under attack even in Paul's day. This is why the first piece of armor he instructs us to put on is the belt of truth.

The Roman Belt

The first piece of armor Paul mentions is the belt of truth. The Roman soldier's belt was a thick leather strap adorned with metal with additional protective straps hanging in the front. The belt held the tunic and breastplate in place, and it held the sword and other important items the soldier needed to have at the ready. In the same way that critical armor such as the breastplate relied on the strength and design of the belt, other key pieces of our spiritual armor fit into—and rely on—the strong foundation of God's truth.

It's no coincidence that in Paul's analogy, the sword of the Spirit (the Word of God) is connected to the belt of truth. Nor is it an accident that the breastplate of righteousness (protecting our heart and emotions) fits into the belt of truth. If God's Word is not true, then we are building our lives on a false foundation. If our heart and emotions are not anchored and submitted to God's truth, they will inevitably lead us into danger.

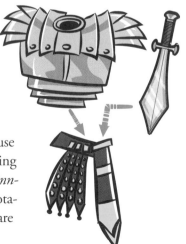

Some Bibles render Ephesians 6:14 as having the belt of truth "buckled around your waist" (NIV), while others render it as "having girded your loins with truth" (NASB). Not many people today use the word *gird*, but it carries some relevant meaning here. The Greek word translated "girded" is *perizónnumi*, and throughout Scripture it carries the connotation of battle readiness. It essentially means "prepare for a physical confrontation." Paul is reminding his readers to be ever ready for the fight. As believers, we must live in a state of readiness. We're already in the battle. We mustn't be caught off guard.

Furthermore, the Greek word translated "waist" or "loin" is *osphus* (os-foos), and it speaks about the reproductive area. The Roman belt had thick leather straps hanging from the front, and some experts believe these were designed to protect the Roman soldier from being taken out of battle due to a strike to this area. There is a reason that martial arts and defense training systems target this vulnerable area when teaching self-defense techniques. An accurately placed strike to the groin can render even the strongest attacker completely immobile.

I share this information because Paul specifically mentions having your loins girded (that is, groin protected). Truth must be intentionally protected. If unguarded, our integrity can be compromised, and this can quickly undermine all the other pieces of armor. Likewise, a strike to any area of foundational biblical truth can gut the rest of the system. For example, the Darwinian theory of evolution has done more damage to the foundational truth of creation than any other modern philosophy. The enemy knows if he can attack the foundation, the rest of the house is on shaky ground. Truth must be protected where it is most vulnerable to the lies of the enemy.

Putting on the Belt

How do we actively engage in putting on our spiritual belt? How does this piece of spiritual armor equip us in real life? For starters, we can make a commitment to being a person of integrity. We should be honest in our dealings, speak the truth, honor the truth, proclaim the truth, and stand for the truth. We should strive to be known as a person of character, honesty, and integrity. This protects us from many of the devil's schemes. Proverbs 20:7 says, "The righteous man walks in his integrity; his children are blessed after him" (NKJV). So there's a general principle that our integrity—or lack thereof—impacts those around us.

In addition to having a personal commitment to truth, I believe it is helpful for the believer in Christ to prayerfully put on their armor each day. This reminds us of where the enemy may attack, how we can protect ourselves from his schemes, and encourages us to recommit our life to God and his ways. It's a practical way to recalibrate our desires and aspirations so they line up with the Lord's purposes for our lives.

Romans 6:11—In the same way, count yourselves dead to sin but alive to God in Christ Jesus.

Paul does not tell us exactly how to put on the armor, just *to* put it on. I'm sure his primary application is that we should make daily choices that line up with God's principles in each area the armor represents. Living in such a way protects us from the enemy's attack plan. He can only attack where he is given an opening by our choices.

With that said, I have heard a few pastors and theologians over the years recommend praying through the armor each morning. I have taken their advice, and I have found it very effective to pray through each piece of armor—envisioning myself putting it on. I don't do it perfectly or consistently every single day—but most days, as part of my prayer time, I pray through each piece of spiritual armor and how it relates to what I'm facing that day. This reminds me of the ever-present war the enemy wages to keep us from God's best. More importantly, it reminds me that my omnipresent loving heavenly Father is watching over me and protects me.

As we prayerfully put on the belt of truth, we should be reminded of the importance of honesty and integrity even in—no, *especially* in—the small things. Small cracks can become gaping holes if allowed to remain. We should also ask the Lord to help us to align our thoughts, motives, and actions with his truth—which is both real and reliable. We should remind ourselves about God's truth in areas where we may be struggling. For example, if you are in a stressful or overwhelming season of life, you will want to recall Bible verses that remind you of God's truth that he will guide you through the day and show you what to focus on, knowing that he has your best interests in mind.

If you are looking around at the world and it seems to be falling apart and causing you to fear, you may need to remind yourself of the truth that Jesus is coming back as promised, that you are here at this moment in history on purpose, and that God has specific things ordained for you to do.

Remember this is *armor*. It is for a battle. The enemy is already attacking. We just need to wake up to the battle and apply each piece of armor for its intended purpose. What truth of God do you need to claim or remind yourself of today? What area of personal honesty and integrity do you need to protect?

Truth is the opposite of lies. That may seem overly simple, but it is profound when you realize the enemy is always lying. Jesus said that lying is Satan's native language (John 8:44). The belt of truth is foundational to the armor because it defends us first where the enemy is always on the attack. He wants to compromise our integrity and our understanding of biblical truth.

Jesus Modeled Truth for Us

When Jesus was spiritually attacked in the desert and faced intense temptation at the hands of the tempter himself, he relied on the truth of God's faithfulness and future promises. Later, just before the cross, when Jesus faced the hard truth of what he was about to suffer, he submitted to the Father's will in the garden of Gethsemane. That enabled him to push through his blood, sweat, and tears. He saw the truth of what he was about to face, but he also saw the truth on the other side of the cross.

Jesus was honest in his rebuke of the political and religious elite even though he knew the hatred and resistance he would face. He proclaimed who he was at the appointed time even though he knew the upheaval it would trigger. He was honest in large and small ways—always letting his integrity dictate his response. Jesus never lied or compromised his integrity—even when it cost him his life.

Through searing pain on the cross, Jesus pushed up on the nail through his feet to catch his breath—but he also pushed up on God's rock-solid truth about what was being accomplished in that moment. Jesus modeled the belt of truth for us in his humanness so that we could have an example to follow in applying truth to real-life circumstances. Though fully God and fully man (a mystery to us for sure), it was in his humanness that he persevered through the horrific events of the cross by standing on God's eternal truth.

Hebrews 4:15—We do not have a high priest who is unable to empathize with our weaknesses, but we have one who has been tempted in every way, just as we are—yet he did not sin.

Belts hold things together. When life goes crazy around us, we can cling to God's truth. Despite our circumstances, we must trust God's Word. Think of stories in the Bible where all seemed lost yet God's plan was still accomplished. The cross was only clear in the rearview mirror. The truth is God has a plan for every battle you face. Jesus said I am the way, the truth, and the life (John 14:6). Let's cling to that truth.

With truth established, it's time to turn our attention to another vital area of human vulnerability—our emotions.

CHAPTER 12

The Body Armor of Righteousness

Above all else, guard your heart, for everything you do flows from it.

PROVERBS 4:23

…and the body armor of God's righteousness.

EPHESIANS 6:14 (NLT)

Is it me, or has Western culture grown increasingly dark, vulgar, violent, twisted, and upside-down in its thinking? That was rhetorical. I know beyond a shadow of a doubt that our times are more immoral and ungodly than when I grew up in the 1970s and 1980s—and it was bad then! As I write this chapter, I have one child in college and two in high school. It is frightening to consider all that bombards and surrounds them through media, culture, political developments, and world conditions. But God prepares a table for us in the presence of our enemies (Psalm 23:5). We can—by faith—be confident that God is still at work in these challenging times.

There are a few biblical figures whose stories can guide us as culture disintegrates into godlessness—figures who lived righteous

lives in spite of the evil culture in which they found themselves. One person I often think of as I consider our era is Daniel. Though he was a captive in a pagan land by an enemy who did their level best to brainwash him—even changing his name to one of pagan origin—Daniel still maintained his faith, integrity, and God-honoring lifestyle regardless of the personal cost.

Another figure who displayed great integrity, righteousness, and self-control was Joseph. Through his roller-coaster life, he stood for righteousness and lived according to godly principles no matter the circumstances. Whether it was literally fleeing from sexual temptation or maintaining his God-honoring faithfulness while in prison for being falsely accused of a crime, Joseph maintained righteousness in his daily choices, whereas most of us probably would have failed.

BILLY GRAHAM

I have always admired the wisdom and forethought of Billy Graham's personal standard of never traveling or staying in a hotel alone. He always had at least one of his male friends with him for some built-in accountability. Even if he could have resisted any temptation that came his way during his frequent travels, the fact that he had an established policy protected him from any potential false accusations, gave his wife and family stability and confidence in Billy's faithfulness to them, and served as a wise guardrail against any temptation the enemy would have loved to send his way.

We are wise to follow Billy's example and place consistent and specific buffer zones between us and sin. None of us are immune to the temptations of the world. We all need to be on guard as we protect ourselves from the unrighteousness all around us.

I Corinthians 10:12—If you think you are standing firm, be careful that you don't fall!

The Roman Body Armor

The second piece of armor Paul mentions in Ephesians 6 is the body armor, which some Bible translations call "the breastplate." The Roman body armor  was made of overlapping iron plates that were fastened together with tough leather straps and brass connectors and weighed approximately 33 pounds. Underneath the armor, the Roman soldier would wear a tunic for padding and to soak up any sweat, blood, or water he encountered during battle. The body armor and the tunic were held in place by the Roman soldier's belt.

In the chaos of battle, soldiers can sustain most wounds to the arms and legs, but an unseen attack from a sword, javelin, or arrow to the torso would usually mean certain death. Vital organs such as the heart, lungs, liver, and kidneys required the highest level of protection from all sides. The Roman soldier's body armor was designed and battle-tested to do just that.

Putting on Our Body Armor

Notice that Paul calls it the "body armor of God's righteousness" (NLT) and not the "body armor of Todd's righteousness." We are first and foremost protected by *God's* righteousness. In Romans 3:10, Paul tells us that "there is no one righteous, not even one." So how do we "put on" righteousness? It is imputed to us through faith. That's a five-dollar word that means God gives it to us. He credits our negative account balance. He pays our sin debt and trades it for his righteousness (2 Corinthians 5:21). That is the great exchange—and it is an absolute

scandal. What King leaves his throne to suffer for the criminals who are against him so that they could become adopted heirs to his kingdom? God does. He trades our filthy rags for spotless clothes.

Though we are *positionally* righteous when we receive Christ, practically speaking, we struggle daily to grow in our righteousness. This is part of our discipleship. As we journey with Jesus, we become more like him. When I think back to how I thought and behaved when I first became a Christian, I am amazed at how drastically the Lord has changed me since then. The Christian life is a journey of growing in our Christlikeness. God's goal is for us to be like his Son.

For the Christian soldier, putting on our body armor means pursuing and protecting personal daily righteousness. It means protecting our purity. This is a polluted world that we have to walk through. The body armor helps us to walk through it as if we were wearing Teflon, not allowing the pollution to stick to us. This must be a conscious daily choice. It is not automatic, and yesterday's decision won't take care of today's temptation. When we mess up, we must be quick to confess and put our body armor back on.

> 1 John 1:9—If we confess our sins, he is faithful and just and will forgive us our sins and purify us from all unrighteousness.

Just as the body armor wraps our entire torso, we must daily clothe ourselves in righteousness. How do we do this practically speaking? Read these instructions from Paul found in Romans 13:13-14 and note how specific and practical they are. Paul advises, "Let us behave decently, as in the daytime, not in carousing and drunkenness, not in sexual immorality and debauchery, not in dissension and jealousy. Rather, clothe yourselves with the Lord Jesus Christ, and do not think about how to gratify the desires of the flesh."

God's righteousness is imputed to us positionally, but we're responsible to put it on practically. We are forgiven and made right with God at salvation, but it is then our responsibility to choose His righteousness in our daily choices. In each tempting circumstance we face, we have one of two choices. We can clothe ourselves with the Lord Jesus Christ. Or we can give in to the desires of the flesh. It's a simple choice, but rarely an easy one. As we grow in Christ, we should see more consistency in making choices toward righteous daily living.

Beware of counterfeit armor. If we're not careful, we can think that checking off boxes equals righteousness. Going to church, tithing, serving in ministry—all of these are good things. But if we are lulled into believing we are righteous because we are checking off behavior boxes, that's self-righteousness. You know what God thinks about our self-righteousness? Not much. In Isaiah 64:6 we read, "All of us have become like one who is unclean, and all our righteous acts are like filthy rags; we all shrivel up like a leaf, and like the wind our sins sweep us away."

God wants genuine, contrite, confessing, raw righteousness. Messy but real is better than polished but fake. We must also keep in mind that we will never live up to God's standard of righteousness. The moment we think we can, we have lost sight of the real distance between our sinfulness and His holiness. Nevertheless, we should strive to grow more Christlike as we mature in our journey.

As I mentioned in the previous chapter, one way to remind ourselves of our responsibility in this area is to prayerfully put on our body armor early in the day—even envisioning ourselves putting it on as we pray. We should pray for protection against influences and circumstances that may tempt us to let our purity guard down.

Protect Your Heart

If you'll recall, the body armor is held in place by the belt. I believe this interplay is relevant to the spiritual armor. Our emotions greatly influence our behavior if we do not guard against this by anchoring our emotions to our personal integrity grounded in the truth of God's Word. What are we drawn to? What excites us? What does our heart beat for?

If our emotions are not submitted to God's truth and personal integrity, they will overflow their banks into dangerous territory. Our emotions can be compared to nuclear energy. They are powerful and productive when properly contained and harnessed for beneficial purposes. But if our emotions are recklessly unleashed toward the pull of the world and our fleshly nature, they lose their proper purpose and can leave massive long-term destruction behind.

For this reason, we must keep our emotions in check. We must guard our gates. If our heart is a city, our eyes and ears are the gates that allow things into our city. We must be very diligent about what we allow through those gates because the enemy has many Trojan horses.

I find it very interesting that in classical Greek education, one key area of training the ancients focused on was the emotions. Students learned about the emotions through the arts. They understood the effect that arts and culture had on one's emotions. In Western culture today, most people don't seem to realize this connection.

Music, paintings, film, and other areas of artistic expression greatly affect our emotions—often without our even realizing it. So it is no wonder that the enemy has deeply infiltrated the arts in our day. Satan and his system of evil influencers attempt to get things through our gates via emotions that would never make it through as a stated fact. In other words, our emotions can easily override truth and sound judgment. They can short-circuit our logic-based decision-making capabilities. I would argue that most (if not all) moral lapses are the result of corrupted emotions and feelings-based decision making.

What else would make someone risk God's blessing, physical health, and the potential for life-long consequences in order to experience momentary pleasure? That is not logic-based thinking but feeling-based nonthinking. Emotions demand immediate gratification. They scream like a spoiled toddler, "I want it now!"

Proverbs 4:23 (at the opening of the chapter) instructs us to guard our hearts above all else. There is a reason for that. This is a critical pass. If the enemy gets past our body armor, he can affect so many other areas. If

we don't guard what our hearts are drawn to, our emotional compromise can trump all other protection.

Jesus Modeled How to Respond Righteously

When Jesus was in the desert and he was offered the kingdoms of the world by the tempter, that was a package deal. Satan wasn't just offering rulership of the kingdoms in a righteous God-honoring way. He was offering Jesus the tempting pleasures and comforts that come with wealth, fame, and power.

I find it very interesting in Scripture that Jesus ministered to many women and had many friendships with women (completely bucking cultural norms and breaking down legalistic walls), but he was never alone with a woman in a private place. He was wise about placing standards or guardrails in place to deny the enemy any room to maneuver. Jesus wisely avoided temptation and even the mere appearance of evil.

A Key to Success

Don't forget the endgame. We must remember that obedience always brings blessing. Enjoying God-created pleasure in a God-honoring way is always better for us in the long run. That is true for time and eternity. Obedience always leads to blessing and future reward. That knowledge should help us in the heat of the battle.

The less spiritually mature we are, the more we focus on the temporal or immediate. The more spiritually mature we are, the more we live for the endgame. If life on earth is a dot on a page and eternity is a continuous line on an endless billboard, why do we so often get caught living for the dot? God has promised in his Word that we have eternal rewards awaiting us. These rewards are directly related to how we live from our position of salvation. Our salvation was free to us, but we work for rewards, and this is a healthy and righteous motivator.

> 2 Corinthians 5:10—We must all appear before the judgment seat of Christ, so that each of us may receive what is due us for the things done while in the body, whether good or bad.

EPHESIANS 6

THINGS TO REMEMBER

Body armor protects our vital organs. Our limbs can be wounded. Even our head can take some damage. But if our heart is pierced, we die on the battlefield. Our emotions should submit to truth. Our heart should beat for the General and his mission. We need to be careful what we are drawn to—it just might be our undoing. Choose today to put on your body armor and to put distance between you and anything ungodly that vies for your emotions or muddies your pure devotion to Jesus. The fight is difficult at times, but being deliberate about putting on your body armor will be more than worth it!

CHAPTER 13

Shoes of the Gospel of Peace

…with your feet fitted with the readiness that comes from the gospel of peace.

EPHESIANS 6:15

When I was about nine years old, I took a trip to visit my mom. She lived in New York and I lived in Maryland. She was back in college studying geology, and I joined her on a field trip of sorts. Her class was studying rock formations in New Jersey. I had no interest in that but loved climbing on the rocks. So while the college students listened to open-air lectures and took notes, I climbed around on the rock formations. It was great fun—at first.

The last stop was a rock formation in Newark, New Jersey, of all places. The city had grown up around the formation, and the area had blocked it off as a city park. Here was a rock formation roughly the size of a quarter of a football field surrounded by bus stops, sidewalks, traffic lights, and store-lined streets. As I was climbing around, jumping from one outcropping to another, I finished trekking across the formation and jumped down onto the city sidewalk that encircled the rock formation. What I didn't notice—until I landed on it—was the broken bottle bottom facing straight up.

I'll spare you most of the gory details, but let's just say the rubber soles of my 1979 Converse Chuck Taylor All Stars were no match for the thick, jagged glass bottle bottom that was now lodged into the bottom of my foot. Needless to say, that was the end of my climbing adventures that day.

When we think of vital areas of our body to protect for survival, we understand how important protecting our head or torso is, but this story reminds us that there is an extremely important area that, if not protected, will stop us in our tracks. If the enemy can steal our peace—either by wearing us down or by the sudden raging storms of life—he can keep us from moving forward in battle. If our peace is stolen, we will find it difficult to keep going in the fight.

We can believe the Bible is true and live a life of integrity. We can avoid the pollution of the world as we put distance between us and temptation. But if we are robbed of our peace, our effectiveness in battle is nullified. So how do we maintain peace in the daily grind and in the storms of life? That is the question we'll answer in this chapter. But first, let's look at the footwear of the Roman soldier.

The Roman Soldier's Footwear

The Roman "sandal" was really more of a lightweight all-terrain army boot with tough leather straps designed to hold them firmly in place, adding strength and stability around the foot and ankle. The bottoms consisted of several thick layers of extremely strong leather. These durable soles were studded with hobnails. In modern terms, a Roman soldier's footwear could be described as extremely tough yet lightweight high-top metal-studded cleats.

The studs kept the leather from wearing out and also helped provide with stability and agility no matter the terrain or weather conditions. The studs on the soles could also be used as a kicking weapon if needed. This footwear was also surprisingly comfortable, enabling soldiers to march for miles on end. Part of the training of the Roman soldier was to complete a nearly 20-mile hike while carrying all of his armor and provisions.

Modern-day soldiers are still trained to understand that a top priority when out in the field is the health of their feet. One blister, infection, or bout with a foot fungus (think athlete's foot), and their effectiveness on the battlefield could be negatively affected. If a soldier's mobility is hampered, it could be a matter of life or death.

Navigating the Mine Field

Satan, the enemy of our souls, has littered the battlefield with perilous traps. Peace-stealing minefields are everywhere, and they threaten our walk. Everywhere we step, there is potential danger. The tempter has spread his evil network and continues to use age-old traps that cater to our fleshly desires in an attempt to trip us up. He has a specific game plan for your personal minefield as well. He knows your weaknesses and wants to exploit them. That is why we need protection as we walk through this world. We know where many of the mines are, and we should try to avoid them.

When I say *he* about our enemy, I'm speaking in a general sense. Satan is not omnipresent, but he uses his evil tiered network of fallen angels to do his bidding. Scripture indicates that as believers, we have guardian angels (Psalm 91:11; Matthew 18:10; Hebrews 1:14). I'm not sure whether they use a man-to-man or zone defense, but perhaps it depends on the level of activity around us. We won't know until we get to heaven how many times angels intervened on our behalf. What we do know is that the minefield is dense. Many are the traps laid that can steal our peace. Thankfully we have help and we have armor. The peace that can be found only in Christ can carry us through the dangerous terrain of this life.

The Source of Our Peace

Once again, the order of the armor is important. Peace comes after righteousness. More specifically, we find peace with God once we are right with him. His imputed (or transferred) righteousness then leads to peace—in the truest sense of the word. We have peace with God, which gives us peace and rest within ourselves.

Jesus talked quite a bit about the peace that the believer can experience in this life while we await the fulfillment of all God has promised to us. In John 14:27, Jesus said, "Peace I leave with you; my peace I give you. I do not give to you as the world gives. Do not let your hearts be troubled and do not be afraid." Then in John 16:33 he talked about peace again, saying, "I have told you these things, so that in me you may have peace. In this world you will have trouble. But take heart! I have overcome the world." Jesus clearly taught that though this world is full of trouble, we can experience peace in the midst of it.

You've heard it said that God is love. God is also peace. Judges 6:24 calls God *Yahweh Shalom*—"The LORD is Peace." In Isaiah 9:6—the famous Christmas prophecy verse—we're told that one of Jesus's names is "Prince of Peace." In Psalm 23:5, we're told that God prepares a feast for us in the presence of our enemies.

In Philippians 4:6-7, Paul gave this powerful promise: "Do not be anxious about anything, but in every situation, by prayer and petition, with thanksgiving, present your requests to God. And the peace of God, which transcends all understanding, will guard your hearts and your minds in Christ Jesus."

The bottom line is that God is the source of true peace. This is taught in the Bible from cover to cover. Nothing else can bring true lasting peace. People try to find peace and rest in a thousand other things: pleasure, work, indulgence, laziness, adventure, risk, control—you fill in the blank. As it has been said, our souls are restless until we find our rest in the Lord. Only a relationship with Christ can bring true peace. Once we have peace with God, we can enjoy the peace of God.

As believers, we are also called to be peacemakers—first and foremost by introducing others to the Source of peace. When we share the gospel, we are inviting people to have peace with God. It is important for us to live with peace even in the midst of chaos. When an unbeliever sees true peace in one of God's children, it is attractive. It speaks louder than words, and the Holy Spirit can use that to draw people to Christ.

We, then, can lead people to peace simply by pointing to the Peacemaker. We can do this by sharing what God has done in our lives. Jesus said, "I, when I am lifted up from the earth, will draw all people to myself" (John 12:32). They may not respond, but the cross is available and appealing to every person who hears about it. There are various reasons why people don't take up Christ's invitation. Our job is not to force a response, but simply to be a witness.

Peace in the Storm

It's one thing to have peace with God. Many new believers, when they first experience this peace, assume that the Christian life is going to be lived on the mountaintop. But then problems come along and bring them back down into the valley. This can shake their peace—and sometimes their faith. A key reason that growing spiritually is so important is because it's our maturity that will enable us to weather the roller-coaster cycle of highs and lows that are part of the Christian life.

Lengthy low-boil trials will either erode the believer's dedication to the battle—or steel their backbone in unfettered determination to go the distance. I pray we all chose the latter. There is a prayer that I have prayed several times in my Christian life and it is this: "Lord, do whatever it takes in this life to keep me close to you." The first time I prayed it, I was literally trembling because I was sincere about my request and I know God answers prayer. I would rather go through hell on earth and stay close to God than live a life of comfort and drift away from him.

When it comes to maintaining our peace, the daily grind is one thing, but what about the storms of life? Christians are not immune to cancer, layoffs, family tragedy, crime, or the many other things that bring sudden overwhelming pain and loss. How are we expected to hold onto our peace in those circumstances?

Fortunately, I have never had a loved one murdered, but I know some believers who have—and they still walk faithfully with the Lord. I have had some storms in life which, before walking through them, I would have wondered if I could make it. Two that come to mind are the sudden loss of my son Ethan when my wife was five months pregnant, and the sudden loss of my mother just a few years ago. In both trials, the enemy was trying to steal my peace. All I can tell you is that in the very darkest moments I sensed God's peace when I needed it the most. The Lord showed up in ways I can't even explain.

I still grieved—I went through all the stages you've heard about. Tears still come to my eyes as I write this chapter. But in the midst of the grief I had (and still have), a deep and abiding peace resides within me that I can't explain. That is why, in Philippians 4:6-7, Paul described God's peace as the peace that "surpasses all understanding" (NKJV).

When going through a sudden and unexpected trial as a believer, the waves on the surface may be roaring, but deep down the water is still calm. Depending on the hurricane category level, you may need to go a bit deeper to find that calmness, but if you know Christ—that peace is still there for you. Don't give up. Just go deeper. We can't do it in our own strength, but God's strength gives us the peace that passes all human understanding.

> 2 Corinthians 12:9—My grace is sufficient for you, for my power is made perfect in weakness.

Putting on the Shoes of the Gospel of Peace

It is important to note that there is a distinction between the first three pieces of armor and the others. They are detailed for us in a single sentence. We're told to stand firm with the belt, body armor, and shoes perpetually on. The remaining three pieces we're told to "take up." And prayer is added as the final key to successfully fighting spiritual battles.

As with the other pieces of the armor, there is action we must choose to take. The default position won't suffice. There is no neutral or resting position in the cosmic war. We must intentionally put on the shoes of the gospel of peace. It is a choice. We must fight for it. Scripture informs us that the enemy is a thief, a liar, and a murderer. He patrols like a roaring lion ready to pounce. We can't get comfortable, but we can actively live in peace.

Yes, we live in a rough landscape. In order to walk through minefields without getting our feet blown off, we need to put on the rugged footwear God gives us to use. It is flexible, tough, stable, and ready for any terrain or temperature. We must take stock in how we are doing in the area of peace. If we sense the enemy has been stealing our peace, we need to recalibrate and intentionally focus on God's promises regarding true inner peace—then fight to maintain it.

Whether marching for our own peace or the peace of others, our spiritual-battle footwear is designed to advance! Retreating or losing ground is not an option. Sure we'll have setbacks, but the overall trajectory of our discipleship or growth in Christlikeness should be one that gains ground and allows us to live in peace—even in the middle of the storm. We should have a net gain in what we've conquered in our lives as we take one step at a time.

Jesus Modeled How to Put on the Shoes of Peace

As the Prince of Peace, Jesus was also the modeler of peace. In his humanness he faced every attack on his peace yet remained faithful to the Father's will.

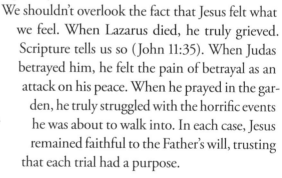

We shouldn't overlook the fact that Jesus felt what we feel. When Lazarus died, he truly grieved. Scripture tells us so (John 11:35). When Judas betrayed him, he felt the pain of betrayal as an attack on his peace. When he prayed in the garden, he truly struggled with the horrific events he was about to walk into. In each case, Jesus remained faithful to the Father's will, trusting that each trial had a purpose.

Jesus also modeled peace for us in other ways during his ministry. In Mark 4:39, Jesus commanded the seas to be at peace. In Mark 5:34, he healed a woman then told her to "go in peace." And in John 20:19, when Jesus first appeared to his disciples in resurrected form, he said, "Peace be with you!"

There is no better peace than resurrection peace! Jesus defeated sin, death, the devil, and everything in between when he rose from the grave. The victory won for us should be our constant focus, for in that victory we find peace. Literally nothing can come against us. Only lies and smoke screens. Tricks and deception. With the help of the armor God has supplied to us, we can deflect those. Our future is secure and we have nothing to fear. Jesus truly is the Prince of Peace. Do you know him? If not, pause here and turn to chapter 19 to learn the ABCs of salvation.

Shoes move people forward. What is one single step toward God you can take today? Prayerfully identify that step and take it. This is doing battle. This is moving the ball forward. This builds momentum and helps provide daily victory over sin, complacency, disobedience, and retreat. Remember, we are more than conquerors in Christ! (Romans 8:37).

CHAPTER 14

The Shield of Faith

*Faith shows the reality of what we hope for;
it is the evidence of things we cannot see.
Through their faith, the people in days
of old earned a good reputation.*

HEBREWS 11:1-2 (NLT)

In boxing, a fighter's defense comes in three primary forms: head movement, foot movement, and a good guard stance. Small head movements that take a fighter's strike zone off the centerline allow them to slip punches. Active footwork creates an elusive target and helps a fighter control range or distance. Both of these forms of defense help create a moving target, but they also create perpetual motion and rhythm. Because it is easier for an object to change direction when it is already in motion, these defensive strategies help a fighter avoid the punches they can see coming. But for the punches they can't see coming—due to the speed, combinations, or effective feints of their opponent—a fighter must rely on a solid and effective guard.

There are various guards that can be used for different situations. The standard guard is a slightly crouched and angled position—chin tucked, arms tight to the body, elbows protecting the liver and kidneys, and the gloves strategically placed to protect the chin. The high guard protects against an onslaught of close-range straight punches to the face and head. An unorthodox defensive stance known as the "Philly defense" can be effective when a fighter is trapped on the ropes or in the corner. Aside from these three guards, there are a few other defensive positions that are used, but less frequently.

A boxer can have a great offense, but if he lacks a good defense, he'll find himself on the canvas rather quickly. There is a very good reason the final instruction a referee gives to fighters just before a match begins is, "Protect yourself at all times." The primary need of a boxer is to have a good defense.

In case you are wondering if you accidentally started reading a book on boxing techniques, here's the connection to the shield of faith: This piece of armor is primarily defensive in nature. It is designed to guard against things you can't plan for or don't see coming—things that are out of your control.

The shield of faith guards against doubt when we have to wait long periods of time to see the fulfillment of the truths and promises we currently accept by faith. It guards against worry and anxiety related to daily struggles and the instability and uncertainty of the world. It guards against the torrents of grief and confusion when hardship or tragedy strikes. And it guards against the hardships of persecution and martyrdom that many believers face today in various parts of Asia, Africa, and the Mideast. Without this key piece of defensive armor, we would not last very long in the battle. Many do not.

The shield of faith has an offensive application as well, and I'll get to that in a moment. For now, let's focus on the primarily defensive nature of this vital piece of armor. But first, a little bit of historical background will help.

The Roman Shield

As part of their battle gear, Roman soldiers carried a large, curved, rectangular shield known as a *scutum*. It had a large iron half-dome (called a *boss*) in the center of the shield. This feature was used for offensive purposes. Roman soldiers practiced using the shield individually for close combat and together in various defensive formations that would be used battle.

The soldiers were trained to align their shields to form 360-degree protection around and above them. By doing this, the soldiers could advance in formation against a barrage of flaming projectiles and remain unscathed. One of the most well-known formations was "the tortoise." This was sort of a Flintstones version of an armored personnel carrier.

This allowed the Roman soldiers to position themselves anywhere on the battlefield regardless of long-range projectile attacks from the enemy.

The Roman shield was made of stitched rawhide over a wooden (or wooden and metal) frame. Soldiers would sometimes soak their shields in water before a battle if flaming projectiles were expected. The wet leather would help extinguish the flames.

Taking Up the Shield of Faith

Regarding the shield of faith in the context of Paul's instructions on spiritual armor, we read this in Ephesians 6:16: "In addition to all this, take up the shield of faith, with which you can extinguish all the flaming arrows of the evil one."

Given the context above about the construction, use, and tactics related to the Roman shield, here are a few key takeaways we can glean from Paul's instructions.

While the belt, body armor, and shoes of the soldier should be perpetually worn, the shield (along with the helmet and sword) are retrieved at certain times when needed for battle. They should always be at the ready in case of an unexpected attack.

The evil one—our enemy, Satan—and his intricate hierarchical system launches flaming spiritual attacks in attempts to keep us pinned down. By faith, we extinguish these fiery projectiles and continue to move forward in battle. The shield of faith allows us to continue advancing into enemy territory.

Together, our shields can lock above and around fellow soldiers for unified protection. But if a soldier is separated from the unit, he becomes more susceptible to enemy attacks. In our Christian walk, we need the fellowship and unity of a local church body. We can't do "solo church" and think that we'll be able to successfully fight the battles we face. Each of us needs a community of believers for mutual accountability, encouragement, and protection. In Scripture, Satan is depicted as a roaring lion (1 Peter 5:8), seeking to devour us. When we drift from our unit, we become vulnerable prey.

Proverbs 27:17—As iron sharpens iron, so one person sharpens another.

What Is Faith?

At this point in our discussion, it may be helpful to answer this key question: Is faith a general belief that "everything happens for a reason"? Is it a matter of willpower, as displayed in various animated movies where characters are told to "wish upon a star" or "just believe"?

Or is true biblical faith based on reason and evidence? I would argue that Christian faith is not blind faith, but a faith based on reason and patterns of evidence. From a purely scientific standpoint, we don't have undeniable proof of our faith. In other words, I can't show God to you. But there is a tremendous amount of evidence that supports all the key aspects of the Christian faith. Note that there is a difference between proof and evidence. Proved facts require no faith. Evidence-based belief does. We're told as much in Scripture, where we learn that "without faith it is impossible to please God" (Hebrews 11:6).

Here's a concrete example: None of us were here when the universe began. The Bible claims to be from God, and it says He created everything in six days. Since we weren't here and do not own time machines, we accept this biblical truth by faith. Yet it is a faith based on reason. This book is not a treatise on Christian apologetics or the evidences for our faith, but there are logical, philosophical, and scientific reasons that support the belief that the Bible is from God and that the universe and everything in it has an intelligent designer.

QUICK FACT: DID YOU KNOW...

that there is an entire field of study known as Christian apologetics that cites logical, historical, archeological, and scientific facts that support the record of Scripture?

Before I became a believer as a young teenager, I wrestled with all these questions. I thought the Bible was a book of fairy tales that were used to control people's behavior, and I believed we evolved "from slime pit to rocket scientist." I had never really thought through what I believed until I was confronted with God's truth—which I had to wrestle with through reason, logic, and seeking truth. When I honestly considered the facts, it was an unexpected game changer.

In other words, I had very real questions regarding the trustworthiness of Scripture and the question of origins. I didn't simply will myself to believe, but I honestly sought truth and followed wherever it would lead. The hundreds (some prophecy experts cite upwards of 2,000) of fulfilled prophecies found in the Bible are convincing evidence that it is divine in nature. Only a being who is bigger than time and truly knows the future could pull that off. This compelling feature, along with other fact-based evidence—such as archeological finds that verify the Bible—were enough to cause me to consider the idea that the Bible really is from God.

The complex and intricate design of the universe from planets to protons forced me to consider the idea that an intelligent, purposeful being created it all. The surprising scientific accuracy of Scripture—long before the scientific age and in stark contrast with other ancient documents and beliefs that were incredibly unscientific—caused me to consider the creation account of origins.

None of the above evidence pushed me over the line of faith, but it caused me to see the reasonableness of the claims and the source. Then I was able to pray—by faith—to the One whom I couldn't see but desired to know, if indeed God was real. The evidence activated my faith, and I began to seek the Creator of the universe and the Author of the Bible. Eventually, this sincere seeking led to my salvation, when I came to believe that Jesus was who he said he was and asked him to save me from the sin that separated me from him.

Worry vs. Faith

With that saving faith in place, believers can face uncertainty with a confidence that God still has his hand on the steering wheel of their lives and the world in which they live. When attacks from the enemy come upon us, trials grind on, layers of stress or turmoil pile on, or sudden tragedy breaks in, our shield of faith helps us to stand firm against the flaming missiles launched our way. The shield of faith protects us from the unknown—from the myriad of "what ifs?"

that could potentially come our way. Rather than live a life of fear and worry, we can walk by faith knowing that God is in control.

Jesus himself spoke powerfully about the inner battle we have between worry and faith. In Luke 12:25-28, he said,

> Who of you by worrying can add a single hour to your life? Since you cannot do this very little thing, why do you worry about the rest? Consider how the wild flowers grow. They do not labor or spin. Yet I tell you, not even Solomon in all his splendor was dressed like one of these. If that is how God clothes the grass of the field, which is here today, and tomorrow is thrown into the fire, how much more will he clothe you—you of little faith!

The Faith Hall of Fame

There's probably no other passage of Scripture that more aptly highlights the importance and impact of faith in the life of the believer than Hebrews chapter 11. It is known as "the Faith Hall of Fame" and it lists some key men and women who demonstrated great faith in the face of major trials. They too had a faith based on reason and evidence. But their faith was tested by the seeming absurdity of the task or trial before them. As Hebrews 11 points out, many of them died a martyr's death, and most of them never saw the object of their faith, or what they were waiting for. But all maintained their faith in the face of overwhelming odds—knowing that their true reward was after this life, when they would finally see the results of their faith.

Hebrews 11:6 contains the baseline for our faith. There, we read, "Without faith it is impossible to please God, because anyone who comes to him must believe that he exists and that he rewards those who earnestly seek him." Then the last couple of verses in the chapter pull us into the continuing story of God's faithfulness: "These were all commended for their faith, yet none of them received what had been promised, since God had planned something better for us so that only together with us would they be made perfect" (verses 39-40).

That's you and me. We are in Hebrews 11. Let's live up to our high calling and focus on our eternal rewards instead of temporary earthly things. By the way, if you have time, pause here and read all of Hebrews chapter 11. It is sure to greatly strengthen your shield of faith and shift your focus from temporary struggles to an eternal perspective.

"We Are Firemen"

There is one detail about the Roman shield that I have purposely waited to highlight—the boss. I mentioned this metal dome feature earlier. This boss allowed the shield to be used as an offensive weapon when a soldier was at close range with the enemy. The blunt-force trauma of the small metal dome served as an effective jabbing weapon at close range.

Perhaps the Lord has given you some insight into his calling on your life. Maybe he's calling you to take back some territory currently held by the enemy. Perhaps you are fighting an addiction or the deceptive strongholds of fear, anxiety, anger, or lust. Or maybe you feel the Lord is calling you to take back territory in cultural strongholds, where you know you will experience great resistance. In these areas, we must step out in faith—and be prepared to mount a strong offense!

Continuing with the boxing theme from the opening of this chapter, I'd like to offer a word of encouragement as you consider your own offensive steps of faith. Knowing that the enemy will continue to launch flaming missiles at you as you follow the Savior into battle, I want to encourage you with a real-life metaphor intended to steel your faith as you stand on the solid ground of God's Word and the leading of the Holy Spirit.

I'm a huge fan of the Rocky movies. Not the later ones, but the earlier films, such as *Rocky* and *Rocky II*. One of my favorite secondary characters is Rocky's trainer, Mick. Mick was one of those iconic old-school boxing trainers who would scream at Rocky in the corner if he wasn't giving his all. Mick was an encourager when Rocky needed building up, but he was a tenacious, in-your-face realist when his fighter wasn't leaving it all in the ring.

ROCKY   MICK

A real-life trainer (and boxing commentator) named Teddy Atlas is the closest thing to a modern-day Mick that I've seen in recent years. In 2015, he coached welterweight champion Timothy Bradley in a title defense match against Brandon Rios. While in the corner between the seventh and eighth rounds, there was a powerful exchange between the weathered trainer and his young champion.

Atlas suspected that Bradley was probably ahead on the judge's score cards, but he also knew the last five rounds of a championship match were the toughest. In even in a remotely close fight, these are the rounds that matter. Here is the transcript of that exchange. As you read it, picture it as a metaphor of your life as you face the challenges ahead and plan to finish strong—with the help of your shield of faith.

Atlas: Can you be strong for fifteen minutes?

Bradley: Yeah.

Atlas: Listen, your concentration is weaving a little bit. Pick it up.

Bradley: (calmly) Okay.

Atlas: (yelling) Pick it up!

[Then Atlas provides a few technical tips.]

Atlas: Look. The fire's comin'. Are you ready for the fire? We're firemen.

Atlas: (yelling) We are firemen!

Bradley: (with a little more energy in his voice) You got it, coach.

Atlas: (yelling) The heat doesn't bother us! We live in the heat! We train in the heat! It tells us that we're ready. That we're at home. We're where we are supposed to be. Flames don't intimidate us! What do we do? We control the flames! We control them. We move the flames where we want to. And then we extinguish them!

Bradley: (enthusiastically) Let's go. Let's go. Let's go![2]

Bradley went on to win the fight two rounds later with a technical knockout.

What about you? Can you take up the shield of faith for defensive and offensive purposes? Will you step into the calling God has for you? If you are already in that fight and growing weary, can you be strong for 15 more minutes? How about 15 more years? By the way, as I'm challenging you, I'm also preaching to myself.

Can we trust by faith that God is working in us, for us, and through us as we take him at his word? Can we take bold and obedient steps of faith into the unknown, trusting that God already has a plan? Can we move forward in faith even if we have to wait until we see Jesus face to face for it all to make perfect sense? If so, perhaps there will be discussions in heaven about our legacy. Perhaps our testimonies will be added to a heavenly Faith Hall of Fame similar to what we read in Hebrews chapter 11.

As we learn to entrust our calling, marriage, family, children, grandchildren, work, health, finances, safety, and future, to God, let's do so with great faith in the One who has proved his faithfulness to us in a thousand different ways.

Jesus Modeled How Take Up the Shield of Faith

Jesus was full of integrity and truth. He was the embodiment of righteousness. And he walked in absolute peace even in the midst of chaos. These qualities were perpetually with him, and as his followers, we need to have the belt, body armor, and shoes of our spiritual armor on at all times.

But there were also moments during Jesus's ministry on earth when he had to take up the shield of faith: approaching John for baptism to begin his ministry, heading to the 40-day test in the desert, choosing 12 frequently knuckleheaded helpers who would later go on to spread the gospel globally, trusting God's plan as miracles and divine words fell on the spiritually deaf ears of the religious leaders of Israel, submitting to the cross and going through a very torturous death. All of these required Jesus to take up the shield of faith. Here are just a few telling statements by Jesus that aptly demonstrate this.

> Matthew 4:2-4—"After fasting forty days and forty nights, he was hungry. The tempter came to him and said, 'If you are the Son of God, tell these stones to become bread.' Jesus answered, 'It is written: "Man shall not live on bread alone, but on every word that comes from the mouth of God."'"

> Matthew 8:26—"He replied, 'You of little faith, why are you so afraid?' Then he got up and rebuked the winds and the waves, and it was completely calm."

Luke 9:58—"Jesus replied, 'Foxes have dens and birds have nests, but the Son of Man has no place to lay his head.'"

Luke 22:42—"Father, if you are willing, take this cup from me; yet not my will, but yours be done."

Luke 23:46—"Jesus called out with a loud voice, 'Father, into your hands I commit my spirit.' When he had said this, he breathed his last."

Shields protect us from powerful long-range weapons and unexpected strikes. We don't know what a day may bring. The shield of faith helps to cover the areas of our life we don't know how to handle. When confusing trials and attacks come our way, we can have faith that God is still in control. Fiery trials can be deflected or extinguished when we raise the shield of faith. When we are under attack we can pray, "God I don't understand this, but I understand enough to know you are still God and you are still in control."

CHAPTER 15

The Helmet of Salvation

We demolish arguments and every pretension that sets itself up against the knowledge of God, and we take captive every thought to make it obedient to Christ.

2 CORINTHIANS 10:5

I don't know exactly how this works in the spiritual realm, but it is clear from Scripture that the enemy has ways of influencing our thinking if we allow him to. As believers we must learn how to recognize an attack from the enemy when it comes, but that is not always easy to do. If you'll recall from an earlier chapter, fallen entities cannot possess believers, but they will certainly try to influence our thinking and oppress us in covert and sometimes overt ways. The enemy is subtle and crafty.

Fallen angels will attempt to leverage our fleshly desires and use them against us. The enemy camouflages his mind attacks so that believers will assume their thoughts and ideas arose from

within. There's nothing more effective than a psy-ops campaign against our thinking so that we don't even realize we are under attack by the enemy.

If I could be very transparent for a moment, I'd like to share a personal story that demonstrates this, sets up the rest of this chapter, and hopefully encourages and equips you in the process. As I was studying for the writing of this book, reading commentaries and rereading an old C.S. Lewis classic on the topic called *The Screwtape Letters*, I experienced some intense spiritual warfare. I guess if you decide to write about this topic with the goal of teaching other Christians how to fight and win spiritual battles, you should expect some level of resistance from the enemy, who desires to keep people in the dark.

C.S. LEWIS

I usually have a positive attitude and an upbeat disposition. I am an encourager by nature, and I generally see the glass as half full. I'm not saying I never get down or that I never think negatively, but most often I am in a good mood and sense God's hand at work in my life. Well, about five months into the writing of this book, I began to experience sudden, short, intense periods of inexplicable discouragement.

During this season of writing I had many other life pressures piled on, but I've had seasons like that before, yet never experienced what was taking place. Trials come and go. Seasons change. I'm not a rookie at dealing with the trials and pressures of life, but something was different this time around—and it was eating my lunch. So I decided to fast and pray.

For 21 days I planned to only eat one meal per day in the evenings with my family. I prayed for breakthrough in the obvious area I was struggling with, but also for several other areas in which I desired to see the Lord move—including the protection of my high school and college-aged children who are growing up in a coarsening culture (2 Timothy 3:1-5) and an increasingly lawless world (Matthew 24:12).

Well, when God's children fast and pray, they often get more than they bargained for. For example, Daniel fasted and prayed to seek God's direction as Israel's 70-year captivity in Babylon drew near to its end, but what he received was much greater that what he expected. God sent an angel to give Daniel the entire history of the Jewish people from his time until the very end, when God would set everything straight (Daniel 9).

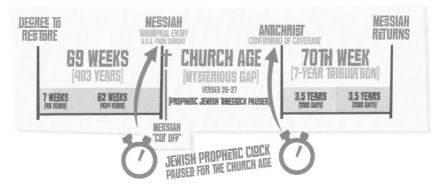

As I prayed for breakthroughs for specific needs, God gave me something much greater. One evening, he woke me up at midnight with the sudden realization that much of the discouragement I was experiencing was due to direct attacks from the enemy upon my thinking. I don't understand the mechanics involved or how the enemy does this from the unseen realm, but it was crystal clear to me at that moment that my recent struggles were a direct result of spiritual warfare.

I can't adequately convey what a breakthrough moment this was, but I knew it would drastically affect how I viewed everything about my calling. As I was absorbing the reality of this truth, I had a split-second image in my mind of me sitting on a stool in the corner of a boxing ring getting punched. I wasn't even putting up my guard—instead, I was sitting there and taking the punches as if that were normal.

If you'll recall from the previous chapter, having a good stance and keeping your guard up are critical to surviving through the rounds. In that split-second image, I stood to my feet with a new confidence and an unhindered realization that I had been taking the enemy's punches on the chin without even realizing that's what was going on and that I could do something about it.

I said out loud (but in a whisper because my wife was sleeping), "No more. I reject anything that is not from God—in the name of Christ." I can't explain it, but this was an absolute game changer—not just related to the discouragement I had been experiencing, but in so many other ways related to my calling, including firming up my commitment to finishing strong no matter what it took or how long it would take. I knew—and the enemy knew—this was a new day.

At the time of this writing, that was several months ago, and the intense discouragement has not returned since. Furthermore, I have a clearer sense of my calling, a greater determination to live for an audience of One, and a grittier commitment to

throw every punch at the enemy I can until the final bell has rung. It all starts in the mind. We renew our mind by soaking it in God's Word (Romans 12:1-2), and what occurs in our mind changes our life.

The Roman Soldier's Helmet

The fifth piece of armor Paul mentions is the helmet of salvation. The Roman helmet was called a *galea*. This custom-fit cranium protector also had guards attached to it that were designed to protect the cheeks and the back of the neck. The helmet was made of metal and designed to withstand the impact of swords or projectiles.

This was the last piece of armor a Roman soldier would put on—the final step as he clothed himself for battle. The helmet was absolutely vital to survival. Protecting the brain was of utmost importance, for it is the command center of all a soldier's faculties. A serious head wound could kill a soldier or leave him so badly injured that continuing to fight was impossible.

Putting on the Helmet of Salvation

Our understanding of salvation and our assurance of its permanence or security are critical for us to maintain. Our grasp of the biblical truths related to our salvation protects us from many attacks of the enemy. Satan is known as the accuser (Revelation 12:10). He and his evil subordinates leverage our past sins and our current imperfections in an attempt to make us question the depth of God's grace. The enemy wants us to think we need to perform at a certain level to gain or maintain our salvation, but it is a free gift—and it is a settled issue for all time. Nothing can take our salvation away from us.

Romans 6:23—The wages of sin is death, but the gift of God is eternal life in Christ Jesus our Lord.

We find in 1 John 5:13 a key proof text that assures us of this fact. There we read, "I write these things to you who believe in the name of the Son of God so *that you may know that you have* eternal life" (emphasis added). If we have accepted Christ, *we know* that *we have* (present tense) eternal life. This may seem redundant when you read it, but I'd also like to point out that eternal life is eternal. Once it starts, it does not stop. Our salvation is not based on our works or continued performance, but upon the settled work Christ did at the cross. Our behavior and spiritual growth then grow out of our secure standing before a holy God.

Romans 8:1—There is now no condemnation for those who are in Christ Jesus.

In addition to having assurance that our relationship with God is reconciled once and for all, there are other important facts that relate to our salvation. We are set free from the power of sin (Romans 8:2); we are indwelt by the Holy Spirit (1 Corinthians 6:19); we have access to God's power (1 Corinthians 1:18); we're part of a new kingdom (Colossians 1:13); we have authority over darkness (1 John 4:4); and we are on the guaranteed winning side (2 Peter 2:4; Revelation 20:10). These facts should shape our outlook as we contend against the darkness that is at work in the unseen realm.

To grow spiritually, we need to soak our minds in the Word of God (Romans 12:1-2). Over time, this helps our thoughts to align with biblical truth. The result is progressively stronger joy, peace, and confidence as we face our battles against the enemy. All of this begins with the mind. Here are few more verses to consider, study, memorize, and apply:

Ephesians 6:17—"Take the helmet of salvation and the sword of the Spirit, which is the word of God."

Colossians 3:2—"Set your minds on things above, not on earthly things."

Romans 12:2—"Do not be conformed to this world, but be transformed by the renewing of your mind, that you may prove what is that good and acceptable and perfect will of God" (NKJV).

2 Corinthians 10:5—"We demolish arguments and every pretension that sets itself up against the knowledge of God, and we take captive every thought to make it obedient to Christ."

Philippians 4:8—"Brothers and sisters, whatever is true, whatever is noble, whatever is right, whatever is pure, whatever is lovely, whatever is admirable—if anything is excellent or praiseworthy—think about such things."

2 Timothy 1:7—"God has not given us a spirit of fear, but of power and of love and of a sound mind" (NKJV).

With all those exhortations in mind (see what I did there?), we should become better equipped to resist the deceptive suggestions of the enemy, maintain a vigilant guard over our minds and desires, reject any thought that does not line up with biblical truth, and make a lifelong commitment to continue strengthening our helmet of salvation.

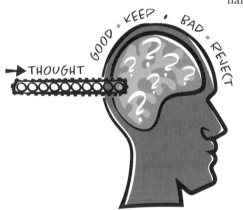

We need to carefully evaluate each thought. If it does not line up with God's Word, God's principles, or God's character, we need to boldly and forcefully reject it—in the name and power of Jesus Christ.

Jesus Modeled How to Put on the Helmet of Salvation

We need to remember that Jesus was 100 percent human—while at the same time 100 percent God. We can't reconcile this in our minds, but the paradox is true. Jesus faced every human temptation, including those that attack the mind.

He clearly did not let fear, lust, comfort, personal agenda, or any other negative thought pattern affect his thinking or attitude. Jesus's 40 days of intense testing in the desert by the tempter himself proved his mastery over the battle for the mind. This prepared him for his three-and-a-half-year earthly ministry in ways you and I don't fully realize.

Before the Father worked through Jesus, he had to work in Jesus via preparation and intense spiritual testing. This testing started first and foremost in his mind. The same is true for us. As we fight the battles of the mind, God is preparing us for future warfare and equipping us to be victorious. We need to develop the mind of Christ, and that requires us to put on the helmet of salvation.

EPHESIANS 6 — THINGS TO REMEMBER

Helmets protect our heads—the thought center of our lives. Our minds are affected by what we allow into our gates—what we see, hear, and touch. Though we can't always control what crosses our gates, we can control what enters them. Just as a body can survive even though it is brain dead, many people go through life as little more than walking zombies. We must determine not to allow the world, the flesh, or the devil to influence our minds. We must purposefully set our minds on things above (Colossians 3:2), have the mind of Christ (Philippians 2:5-8), take every thought captive (2 Corinthians 10:5), and dwell on the things that honor God (Philippians 4:8). Our helmet will be thick or thin based on our choices. When we fail, we must be quick to repent (1 John 1:9) and put our helmets back on. While we are here on earth the battle will never stop— but whatever effort we put forth toward standing strong will all be worthwhile when we trade our helmets for eternal crowns.

CHAPTER 16

The Sword of the Spirit

The word of God is alive and active. Sharper than any double-edged sword, it penetrates even to dividing soul and spirit, joints and marrow; it judges the thoughts and attitudes of the heart.

HEBREWS 4:12

If you'll recall from chapter 11, I noted that attached to the belt of truth was the sheath for the sword of the Spirit. Truth and God's Word are connected. In fact, in John 17:17, Jesus plainly and boldly stated to the Father, "Your word is truth." They are one and the same.

God's Word sets addicts free, changes the hearts of evil people, transforms culture, rescues families, guides history, and demonstrates God's faithful character. It is also constantly under attack by those who hate it. Atheists, humanists, progressive pundits, and scientists with lots of letters after their names have dedicated themselves to discrediting, dismantling, and disproving the Bible. Paul the apostle informs us that "God chose the foolish things of the world to shame the wise; God chose the weak things of the world to shame the strong" (1 Corinthians 1:27). Yet those who search diligently for the truth with an open mind will find it, such as former atheist Lee Strobel, who became a Christian and went on to write the bestseller *The Case for Christ*.

The famous French philosopher Voltaire, who was critical of Christianity, once said this about the Bible: "A hundred years from my death the Bible will be a museum piece."[1] Well, guess what? Voltaire died in 1778, and the Bible is still the all-time bestselling book on the planet. In fact, 100 years after Voltaire's death, the French Bible Society set up its headquarters in his old home in Paris. From that very location they printed Bibles to ship all over Europe.

> Psalm 119:89—Your word, LORD, is eternal; it stands firm in the heavens.

Though the Bible was written by at least 39 authors from 3 continents over a period of 1,500 years, it tells one complete story. There are no contradictions, scientific mistakes, historical inaccuracies, or failed prophecies. If someone tells you there are, you can be certain there is an answer for the claim. We have many great resources today that help provide clear explanations for the so-called errors or mistakes—some great places to start are *The Harvest Handbook for Apologetics* by general editor Joseph Holden, *The Historical Reliability of the New Testament* by Craig Blomberg, *Evidence That Demands a Verdict* by Josh and Sean McDowell, and *The Big Book of Bible Difficulties* by Norman Geisler and Thomas Howe.

Under careful examination, many of the allegations against the Bible come down to failures to consider a passage's context, examine the full historical evidence, correctly interpret the original languages or the intent of a passage, or some other aspect of careful Bible study. Every generation has those who attempt to undermine, discredit, destroy, or minimize the Bible—but it is God's eternal Word, and it will stand forever. No other book in history has had the impact that the Bible has had on the world.

> 1 Peter 1:25—The word of the Lord endures forever.

The Roman Sword

The Roman soldier's sword was an offensive and defensive weapon. It was known as the *gladius*. It was not long, but rather, short and double-edged (blades on both sides), designed for close combat. The smaller size and construction also made the sword light. These characteristics allowed soldiers to use the sword with speed and tactical precision in close combat. It worked well for quick thrusts or slashing in any direction.

QUICK FACT: DID YOU KNOW...

the only place in Scripture that the sword of the Spirit is mentioned is in Ephesians 6, where Paul talks about the full armor of God?

The Holy Spirit

Scripture clearly tells us this final piece of spiritual hardware is "of the Spirit" (Ephesians 6:17). That makes sense, for God's Word was inspired by the Holy Spirit—the third person of the Trinity. Though He did not physically pen the words, the Holy Spirit supernaturally inspired the writings of the Bible (2 Timothy 3:16-17) as he spoke through those who wrote it (2 Peter 1:21).

The sword of the Spirit, then, is supernaturally powered, ordained of God, eternal, and life-changing. Hebrews 4:12 (cited at the opening of this chapter) calls it "alive." It penetrates deep enough to divide "soul and spirit," which is another way of saying it can pierce our innermost being.

Jesus Modeled How to Use the Sword of the Spirit

Each time Jesus was tempted in the desert, he fought back with the Word of God with surgeon-like precision. When the starving Messiah was tempted to misuse his divinely restrained power to turn stones into fresh, hot bread, he used the sword of the Spirit. He slashed at the tempter with the words of Deuteronomy 8:3 when he said, "Man shall not live on bread alone, but on every word that comes from the mouth of God" (Matthew 4:4).

When the enemy used Jesus's vulnerable condition to temp him to glorify himself instead of submitting to the Father by jumping off of the temple into the unseen arms of protecting angels, Jesus fought back with the words of Deuteronomy 6:16: "It is also written: 'Do not put the Lord your God to the test'" (Matthew 4:7).

When Lucifer came a final time, tempting Jesus with the prestige, power, and privilege that came with all the kingdoms of the world in exchange for worshiping the enemy, Jesus once again unsheathed the sword of the Spirit and quoted Deuteronomy 6:13: "Away from me, Satan! For it is written: 'Worship the Lord your God, and serve him only'" (Matthew 4:10).

Taking Up the Sword of the Spirit

Notice that Jesus was prepared offensively and defensively. He knew the Scriptures. He had memorized them. He had spent time studying, internalizing, and meditating on God's Word so that when the time of testing and tempting came, he had a well of powerful truths to draw upon. Jesus never ceased to be God, but he lived out his life on earth—including when he went through severe testing—in his humanness. Though we may get brain cramps when we try to figure out this mystery, it remains true: Jesus was fully God and fully man.

It is amazing to see the precision by which Jesus used the sword of the Spirit. This comes only by training and preparation. Jesus is our model as well as our Savior. The goal of our personal discipleship is to become more like him. He showed us how to use the sword of the Spirit so that we would follow suit.

Just as the Roman soldier trained with the sword—and just as Jesus prepared for the moments he would need the sword of the Spirit—so must we train with the Word of God. We need to go to Bible boot camp, then continue with special-ops Scripture school. There are no shortcuts. We must study and memorize God's Word as believers.

Acts 17:11—Now the Berean Jews were of more noble character than those in Thessalonica, for they received the message with great eagerness and examined the Scriptures every day to see if what Paul said was true.

In 2 Timothy 2:15, Paul exhorts every believer to "do your best to present yourself to God as one approved, a worker who does not need to be ashamed and who correctly handles the word of truth." Here's the TPV (Todd's paraphrase version) take on that verse: "Be ready to stand before God knowing you've put in the work with the Word. Train hard so you won't be embarrassed by handling a deadly weapon in a clumsy and careless way. Work hard to be proficient with the sword of the Spirit. Never stop training!"

Christian, don't be satisfied with a children's picture-book Bible knowledge. Dig deeper. Do the work. Remember, we're not on a field trip; we're on a battlefield.

The enemy is working overtime to eliminate you from the equation, but you have protection. Practice daily with the sword. The more you study God's Word, the more you will fall in love with it. Also, you are what you eat, so the more you digest God's Word, the more it becomes a natural part of you. That's why Jesus didn't have to go find his Bible or pause before striking the enemy with the sword of the Spirit. Scripture was a natural part of who he was.

We live in an era when there are more Bible study tools available than any other time in history, yet surprisingly, ours is a biblically illiterate generation. So, what can you and I do to combat this trend and ensure we are not a part of it? Here are a few steps we can take:

- memorize Scripture
- use a Bible app or subscribe by email for a daily reading
- set a goal to read through the entire Bible chronologically
- pick a topic that confuses you and study it in depth
- develop a list of verses related to problem you struggle with
- pick a relevant verse and use an online lexicon to do a word study

Select Verses to Memorize or Study

In addition to the verses cited earlier in this chapter, here are a few more key verses related to sharpening your sword:

> Job 23:12—"I have treasured the words of his mouth more than my daily bread."

> Psalm 12:6—"The words of the LORD are flawless, like silver purified in a crucible, like gold refined seven times."

> Psalm 119:11—"I have hidden your word in my heart that I might not sin against you."

> Psalm 119:105—"Your word is a lamp for my feet, a light on my path."

> John 1:1—"In the beginning was the Word, and the Word was with God, and the Word was God."

> 2 Timothy 3:16—"All Scripture is God-breathed and is useful for teaching, rebuking, correcting and training in righteousness."

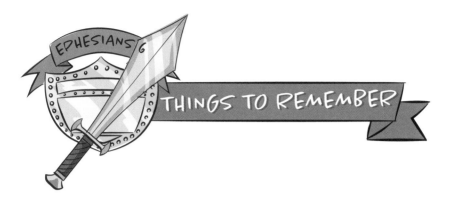

EPHESIANS 6

THINGS TO REMEMBER

Swords cut and chop. They penetrate more effectively than any other weapon. They cut both ways—offensively and defensively. Swords are sharp, but they are effective only when used. They can seem foreign to our hands if we don't practice using them, or they can feel like an extension of our bodies if we do. No enemy can defend against the sword when it is wielded by dedicated hands. A strategic and skilled swing of the sword can slay giants.

We need to practice our swordplay daily and keep this weapon ready at all times. The soldier of God never knows when an attack is coming—only *that* it is coming. Training comes before battle, so we must always train. We can never overprepare in our use of the sword of the Spirit. We can always get better.

CHAPTER 17

Prayer

Pray in the Spirit on all occasions with all kinds of prayers and requests. With this in mind, be alert and always keep on praying for all the Lord's people.

EPHESIANS 6:18

The various branches of the US military have special operations forces. These are made up of units of soldiers who have been specially trained to tackle the most risky and dangerous military operations in the world—most of which are never heard about by the general public.

Special-ops forces such as the Navy SEALs, Army Green Berets, Marine RECONs, and Air Force Special Tactics are comprised of the most elite soldiers in the world. Their training is beyond rigorous, and the qualifications to join such exclusive groups of warriors are extremely high. These elite soldiers make up a small percentage of the total military, but they are the tip of the spear when it comes to critical combat operations.

These units usually operate in small numbers, drop behind enemy lines, practice tactics repetitively before executing a given operation, and train for every combat condition they might encounter. But even with an exceptional level of training and expertise, there is one critical component that is absolutely necessary for them to successfully reach their objective: communication.

These elite special-ops fighters are part of a larger overarching entity with which they must stay in communication—SOCOM. This acronym stands for Special Operations Command.[1] Key to their success from the elite soldier on the field all the way to the commander-in-chief is communication through SOCOM.

A unit or soldier on mission in the theater of battle can have the latest weapons and technology, but they cannot access the fuller power and might of the military without the critical link—communications. If a satellite phone goes down or can't access a signal, this life-or-death communication is broken. Without the ability to call in for air support when being overrun, medical evacuation when someone is injured, or passing on key intelligence information to SOCOM, an operation can be compromised. When communication is absent, things can go south in a hurry. In the realm of special military operations, communication is life.

As we train with our spiritual armor, we must remember to keep the communication lines with SOCOM (Supernatural Operations Command) open, and we must remember to communicate early and often with the Lord. We can keep the communication lines open by following God's ways, turning from ungodly ways, and confessing sins quickly. We access the strength, wisdom, will, and heart of God by communicating with him regularly as we battle.

Though people often don't think of prayer as part of the believer's armor, it is arguably the most important part of it. Prayer is the means by which we access all the other armor. Without relying on God's power, we're simply fighting in our own strength. We must seek His strength rather than depend on our own. The way we do this is primarily through prayer, followed by trust.

Trying to fight battles without prayer is like trying to drive a car without gasoline, or trying to scuba dive without an oxygen tank. It is make-or-break. It is that important. I'm personally convicted even as I write this paragraph. I need to step up my communication with SOCOM.

Roman Communications Technology

Much like their modern-day special-ops counterparts, Roman soldiers used the latest technology of the time. Though you and I may not consider the Roman road system, signaling (with the use of flags from a distance), runners, hilltop bonfires, and other ancient Roman communications methods as technology, these were cutting-edge communications systems at the time.

You and I are accustomed to instant communication via modern technologies such as cell phones, texting, and video chat. These technologies are such an everyday part of our lives that we

KEY COMMUNICATIONS MILESTONES [2,3,4]

1844 Telegraph
1876 Telephone, phonograph
1894 Wireless telegraph
1922 Radio broadcasts
1940 Black-and-white TV broadcasts
1945 Modern computers
1953 Color TV broadcasts
1954 Transistor radios
1962 Satellite communications
1983 First cell phone
1992 First smartphone
1996 Vast expansion of the Internet
1999 High-speed Internet
2005 YouTube
2008 YouTube Live

often forget they are fairly recent developments. For thousands of years, communicating over large distances was a slow, cumbersome process. It is only in our modern era that instant communication has been made available.

Approaching God's Throne

Even though instant communication in the natural realm is only a recent development, talking directly to God through a relationship with Christ has been available for nearly 2,000 years. Jesus's death and resurrection opened up a direct communication link between Creator and creation.

Those of us who have received Christ can go directly to God. We don't need the help of a priest. The cross removed the middleman. We now have direct access to the throne of grace (Hebrew 4:16). As believers in Jesus Christ, the Bible informs us that we are chosen, royal priests.

> 1 Peter 2:9—You are a chosen people, a royal priesthood, a holy nation, God's special possession, that you may declare the praises of him who called you out of darkness into his wonderful light.

At times we take it for granted what a privilege it is to be able to pray directly to the Creator of all things. He has demonstrated his compassionate love for us by sending his only Son to die for us on the cross. Unlike the lowercase-*g* gods of other religions, the one true God is a deeply personal being who offers eternal life and longs to maintain an intimate, ever-deepening relationship with his children.

This may at times cause us to forget that we must also approach him with great care In addition to being told we can boldly approach God's throne of grace, Scripture also reminds us to have a reverent, respectful fear of God (see Proverbs 9:10; Hebrews 12:28-29). Not the kind of fear that anticipates a terrible fate, but a deep awe and respect for the righteous character and might of the Creator.

Don't let the scoffers who twist the meaning of Scripture make you think we should fear a capricious, moody, or irrationally violent God. When the Bible instructs us to fear God, it is teaching us to maintain a healthy awe and respect for what he has done, what he is capable of, and what he is going to do.

We should have a healthy fear of going against God's will because there are fixed spiritual consequences. I've been whitewater rafting a few times, and it is wise for everyone in the raft to have a healthy fear of the power of moving water. When our guide led us through class IV and class V rapids, I listened carefully to his instructions so I could steer clear of danger and emerge unscathed once the rapids were past. On a much larger scale, we should maintain a healthy respect and awe for the God who made the rapids, the river, the earth, and the universe.

Practicing Our Prayer Tactics

Just as the Roman soldier had to learn how to communicate on the battlefield, we must learn to communicate with God in our daily battles. Here are some key verses about prayer and some practical applications to consider.

Antidote to Anxiety

> Philippians 4:6-7—"Do not be anxious about anything, but in every situation, by prayer and petition, with thanksgiving, present your requests to God. And the peace of God, which transcends all understanding, will guard your hearts and your minds in Christ Jesus."

These divinely inspired words teach us that the antidote to worry is taking our concerns to God in prayer and leaving them there. Worry is the opposite of trust. My first pastor used to say, "Worry is a Christian sin." When we worry, we are living as practical atheists—refusing to trust the God in whom we say we believe. As believers, we must practice the tactic of taking our specific worries, needs, and anxieties directly to the Lord. As we do this with a thankful attitude and implicit trust, our worry will be replaced with supernatural peace.

Prayer Changes Us, Not God

1 John 5:14—"This is the confidence we have in approaching God: that if we ask anything according to his will, he hears us."

We learn from this short but powerful verse that our will must be submitted to God's will, and our motives must be right when we come to him in prayer. Much of our wrestling in prayer should be spent aligning our will to that of the Father's. He is holy and perfect. We are fallen yet redeemed and growing. Teenagers often think they know more than their parents, but sometimes painful reality proves otherwise. I thought I was so much smarter than my dad when I was a teenager, but by the time I got to my mid-twenties, I realized he was much smarter than I thought. Similarly, we dare not make the mistake of thinking we know better than God.

Mutated Motives

James 4:2-3—"You desire but do not have, so you kill. You covet but you cannot get what you want, so you quarrel and fight. You do not have because you do not ask God. When you ask, you do not receive, because you ask with wrong motives, that you may spend what you get on your pleasures."

Because we still inhabit fallen bodies, even as believers our motives can get clouded by desires for the things of this world. Like the psalmist, we must invite God to search our hearts and test us to reveal any impure motives we might have (Psalm 139:23). As God realigns our motives and desires to line up with the things that are important to him, we can ask in confidence for his help.

Constant Communication

1 Thessalonians 5:16-18—"Rejoice always, pray without ceasing, in everything give thanks; for this is the will of God in Christ Jesus for you" (NKJV).

We should develop a habit of continual prayer that comes from a thankful and joyful heart. Thankfulness and joy are choices that result in emotion, not the other way around. Prayer is more of an established posture than a momentary event.

God's Throne of Grace

Hebrews 4:16—"Let us then approach God's throne of grace with confidence, so that we may receive mercy and find grace to help us in our time of need."

Last, don't get bogged down in formulas. God made a way through the cross. Grace is God's unmerited favor offered to those who put their trust in Christ. God is not a puzzle to be unlocked; he is a safe place to collapse into, a shelter in the storm, and a Father to run to. Sometimes we can make coming to God in prayer much more complex than it needs to be. There's a comical yet poignant poem called *The Prayer of Cyrus Brown*, written by Sam Walter Foss (1858–1911), which highlights the power and simplicity of a desperate and sincere prayer.

"The proper way for a man to pray,"
 Said Deacon Lemuel Keyes,
"And the only proper attitude,
 Is down upon his knees."

"No, I should say the way to pray,"
 Said Reverend Dr. Wise,
"Is standing straight with outstretched arms,
 and rapt and upturned eyes."

"Oh, no; no, no," said Elder Snow,
"Such posture is too proud:

A man should pray with eyes fast closed
and head contritely bowed."

"It seems to me his hands should be
Asterely clasped in front,
With both thumbs a pointing toward the ground,"
Said Reverend Doctor Blunt.

"Las' year I fell in Hodgkin's well
Head first," said Cyrus Brown,
"With both my heels a-stickin' up,
my head a-p'inting down;
"An' I made a prayer right then an' there—
Best prayer I ever said,
The prayingest prayer I ever prayed,
A-standing on my head."[5]

God hears short prayers, long prayers, desperate prayers, small-need prayers, big-need prayers, and everything in between. The issue is not what formalities we use, but the heartfelt desperation behind our prayers and the specificity of our requests.

Jesus Modeled How to Pray

Jesus lived a life of prayer, and he modeled it by praying alone and "often" with his disciples (John 18:2). He submitted to the will of the Father and brought his specific needs to him in prayer. He also gave us a model of how to pray through what is commonly referred to as the Lord's Prayer.

Jesus's model prayer is found in Matthew 6:9-13:

> This, then, is how you should pray: "Our Father in heaven, hallowed be your name, your kingdom come, your will be done, on earth as it is in heaven. Give us today our daily bread. And forgive us our debts, as we also have forgiven our debtors. And lead us not into temptation, but deliver us from the evil one."

Volumes have been written on this short prayer, but for our purposes, I'll point out just a few things. First, Jesus opened the prayer by acknowledging and admiring the God who lives in heaven and whose name should be held in high honor. Then he prayed for God's will, and for God's promised prophetic future to arrive. Then after affirming God's majesty and praying for the culmination of his ordained plan to come in its fullness, he turned to his specific daily spiritual and physical needs, including forgiveness and protection against temptation and the spiritual warfare this book is about.

QUICK FACT: DID YOU KNOW...

if you need a simple method to kickstart your prayer life, you can use the ACTS method? That stands for Adoration, Confession, Thanks, and Supplication (bringing your needs and the needs of others to God).

Jesus also modeled how to persevere in prayer in the toughest of circumstances. On the Mount of Olives on the night of his arrest—knowing all that he was about to endure—Jesus went a distance away from his disciples so he could pray alone with the Father. We read in Luke 22:41-44,

> He withdrew about a stone's throw beyond them, knelt down and prayed, "Father, if you are willing, take this cup from me; yet not my will, but yours be done." An angel from heaven appeared to him and strengthened him. And being in anguish, he prayed more earnestly, and his sweat was like drops of blood falling to the ground.

That is the target we're shooting for—praying with the same kind of earnestness. We'll never reach it, but we should aim for it. We should strive to be more like Christ in our prayer life as we submit to God's will no matter how difficult life gets. We should persevere in prayer even when we don't see how God is going to work through a given circumstance.

Those are the kinds of prayers that make the enemy tremble and crack the foundations of evil strongholds. Those are the kinds of prayers that make the rest of our spiritual armor effective. Those are the kinds of prayers that enable us to tap into God's strength so that we can do battle in the theater of spiritual warfare.

Prayer cracks the foundations of stronghold and sets the battle plan in motion. Going to battle without prayer is like entering a war with no cover. We can't go rogue. Through prayer we bring the assets of heaven into place on the battlefield. Communication is the most vital combat weapon. Without it there is no coordination—only confusion.

SECTION 4:

ENTERING THE BATTLE

CHAPTER 18

Spiritual Warfare in the End Times

The hour has already come for you to wake up from your slumber, because our salvation is nearer now than when we first believed. The night is nearly over; the day is almost here. So let us put aside the deeds of darkness and put on the armor of light.

ROMANS 13:11-12

When my wife and I first learned we were going to have a child, I decided to start a journal that would commemorate our child's birth, then record stories and milestones in a birthday entry each year. My goal was to complete an entry each year until he turned 18 (or graduated from high school—whichever came first). The journal would have 20 entries total: an initial entry, an entry for his spiritual birth when he accepted Christ (we prayed), and then one entry for each birthday. Once all 20 entries were completed, I planned to give it to him as a graduation gift.

Thankfully I followed through on that plan, and I'm doing the same now for my other two children. As I write this chapter, my oldest son is in college, I have one more entry to go in my daughter's journal, and I have four more entries to go in my youngest son's journal. It seems like just a few years ago that I wrote the first entry in the first journal, but before I knew it, 18-plus years have passed—seemingly in the blink of an eye.

Early on, it seemed that eons would pass before I would be able to present the first journal to my first child. I pondered what that moment would be like. In my glamorized anticipation of this future event, I imagined him tearfully offering a grand speech about how meaningful the journal was and how powerful this prayerfully written record of his early milestones would be in his life.

Before I knew it, that moment snuck up on me like a pickpocket on a crowded city street. The giving of the journal didn't happen quite how I had imagined, but it came to pass, and time has not slowed since. In fact, the older I get, the faster time seems to go!

In Scripture, we learn a lot about spiritual warfare as we study the roughly 7,000 verses of fulfilled Bible prophecies, as well as the numerous future prophecies that have yet to be fulfilled. The 100 percent "literal fulfillment" rate of these detailed prophecies assures us that the remaining prophecies will also be fulfilled literally.

Here's the first kicker: End-time Bible prophecies are directly connected to spiritual warfare. More prophecies are dedicated to the future seven-year tribulation than to any other time period of history. Think about that for a moment. This period is known as the Day of the Lord, Daniel's seventieth week, the Time of Jacob's Trouble, the tribulation, the time of travail, and a few other terms. This intense future period will see the culmination of thousands of years of spiritual warfare. During that time, the seen and unseen realms will collide like never before.

Here's the second kicker: All the sign indicators described in Scripture point to the fact that we are very close to this prophesied period. Many Bible prophecy experts agree that you and I are living in the closing moments of the church age. In my book *The Non-Prophet's Guide™ to the End Times*, I spent seven full chapters detailing the biblical veracity and current reality of end-time signs unfolding in our day. Beginning with the supersign of Israel's rebirth as a nation (a prerequisite for all other end-time events), and ending with the convergence of specific end-time signs and conditions taking place right now, we can be quite confident that we are living in the season of the Lord's return and the soon fulfillment of key end-time Bible prophecies.

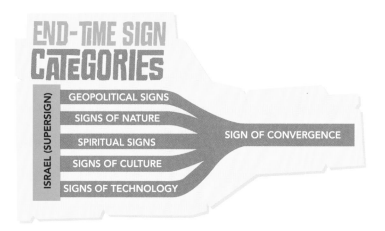

Prophecies that believers have studied for almost 2,000 years have snuck up on us, but many are not aware of this reality. The church at large is asleep to the fact that the paranormal is about to become the new normal. Covert spiritual battle tactics will soon give way to overt spiritual warfare unlike anything the world has ever seen. Are you ready? It's time to polish our armor and suit up. Things are about to change.

Looking Back: Recapping What We've Learned

Here is a brief summary of the historical and theological points we've covered in this book. Reviewing these key plot points will help us to recognize how certain aspects of spiritual warfare affect us today as we near the end of the church age.

A CONDENSED HISTORY OF SPIRITUAL WARFARE

- Eternity past—God is self-existent
- God creates heavenly beings (*elohim*)
- God creates physical universe—six days of creation
- Eden/paradise of God—seen and unseen realms seem to overlap (*probable location of divine council*)
- Lucifer and one-third of the heavenly beings rebel
- Adam and Eve tempted/fall of mankind
- First prophecy of a future Messiah (Genesis 3:15)

- "Seed war" ensues
- Corruption of the human genome/Nephilim (Genesis 6)
- Global deluge/Noah's flood
- Fallen angels who sinned in Genesis 6 imprisoned in Tartarus
- Tower of Babel—Nimrod attempts fallen version of Eden
  (Gateway to unseen realm/roots of globalism and the occult)
- Nimrod's genome changed
- God stops Babel/divides the nations/confuses languages
- God chooses Israel as his own nation/people
- Babylon becomes the first of four key empires
- The occult spreads with each empire
- Angels shown to oversee geographical areas (Daniel)
- Afterlife shown to have compartments for righteous and
  unrighteous dead
  (Paradise and Hades—also Tartarus/Abyss/bottomless pit)
- Very active demonic season during Jesus's earthly ministry
  (Jesus displays authority over demons—some sent into bottomless
  pit/Tartarus)
- Jesus's three-day trip to Hades/abode of the dead
  (Moves Paradise to heaven/showed the Genesis 6 fallen angels they
  had legally failed)
- Christians in church age caught in middle of the war (Ephesians 6)
- Spiritual warfare climaxes in future seven-year tribulation period
  (and one final battle at the end of the millennial kingdom)

Looking Forward: Understanding What Is Coming

With that overview of key spiritual warfare plot points as a backdrop, let's shift gears and look to the future and study what Scripture reveals about spiritual warfare at the time of the end. As the church age winds down and the end-time birth pains Jesus spoke of in Matthew 24:8 ramp up, we need to be informed about what is ahead. All past prophecies were fulfilled literally and accurately. We should expect all future prophecies to be fulfilled in like manner.

With that approach as our guide, here are some key spiritual warfare events that will take place in the future—the first of which will be the rapture of the church. This will be the domino that sets all the other dominos in motion.

You may be surprised to hear me refer to the rapture as a spiritual warfare event, but it is. I talked about this briefly in an earlier chapter. The rapture will be a wonderful event for believers, but it will also be a special-ops snatch-and-grab in the heart of enemy territory. Satan is called the ruler of the kingdom of the air (Ephesians 2:2). Jesus himself will invade Satan's territory—in the middle of the air—and rescue his own before the most horrifying time the planet has ever seen takes place.

The rapture is a signless and imminent event. It can occur at any moment with no preconditions. The enemy knows this game-changer is coming, but he doesn't know when. Satan also knows there is nothing he or his minions can do to stop it. Therefore, Satan has been laying the groundwork for his end-time counterattacks for almost 2,000 years. There are several strategies the enemy has employed in order to prepare the world for a great deception the moment the church (indwelt by the Holy Spirit) is removed from planet Earth. The preserving qualities of salt and the evil-exposing nature of light will be taken out of the equation "in a flash, in the twinkling of an eye" (1 Corinthians 15:52). A tidal wave of deceptive evil will quickly flood the void.

For a thorough overview of the order of end-time events as well as the strengths and weaknesses of the various views about the end times, please refer to my book

The Non-Prophet's Guide™ to the End Times. There, I highlight the need for unity in the body of Christ even if we disagree on our end-time views. I also lay out what I consider to be the overwhelming strength of a literal futurist interpretation of end-time Bible prophecy and the pretribulational/premillennial rapture of the church.

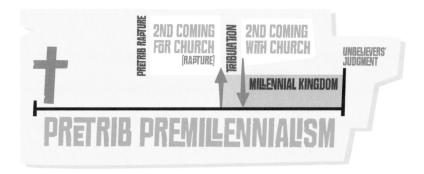

In my book *The Non-Prophet's Guide™ to the Book of Revelation*, I take that approach and study each chapter of Revelation and describe the 21 judgments (and many other details) of the coming tribulation. Space limitations do not allow for an in-depth overview here, but I want to point out a few key themes that specifically relate to spiritual warfare during the tribulation.

Globalism with a One-World Ruler

Since the Tower of Babel, various figures and groups have pushed for a one-world government. During the future tribulation period, this diabolical dream will finally come to fruition when a dynamic figure known as the antichrist will emerge in the aftermath of the rapture. He will rise to power as an apparent peacemaker—a fix-it man whom the world believes will bring order out of chaos. Boy, will they be wrong!

This end-times world leader will impress the masses with great signs and wonders in a deceptive bid to receive the reins of power. The books of Daniel, 2 Thessalonians, 1 John, and Revelation provide many details about this future deceiver. He is foreshadowed by Nimrod and Nebuchadnezzar, the key Babylonian figures of the past. This ultimate evil despot will make Hitler look like Mr. Rogers. Billions will die during his rule.

WHO IS THE ANTICHRIST?

"the little horn"	**Daniel 7:8**
"a fierce-looking king"	**Daniel 8:23**
"a master of intrigue"	**Daniel 8:23**
"the ruler who will come"	**Daniel 9:26**
"a contemptible person"	**Daniel 11:21**
"a shepherd who will not care"	**Zechariah 11:16**
"a worthless shepherd"	**Zechariah 11:16-17**
"man of lawlessness"	**2 Thessalonians 2:3**
"the lawless one"	**2 Thessalonians 2:8-9**
"the rider on the white horse"	**Revelation 6:2**
"a beast"	**Revelation 13:1**

The reign of this end-times figure will prove that globalism is not a good thing. While secular humanism does not account for the inherent fallen nature of mankind, the total depravity of our sin nature will be on full display in violent global conquest. The enemy is after a counterfeit kingdom and global worship. God's post-Babel establishment of separate nation-states continues to keep the enemy's globalist agenda at bay. All of that will change in the wake of the rapture. Then Satan's end-times ruler will rise to global power and dominate the world for a brief and horrific time.

Some Bible expositors note the fact that Genesis 3:15 is not only the first prophecy of the coming Messiah, but possibly the first prophecy of the end-times antichrist as well. In addition to the woman's seed/offspring (singular context), there is also the serpent's seed/offspring. While the word "seed" can be understood as either singular or plural depending on the context, the second part of the verse lets us know that the woman's seed (referred to as "he") is understood to be singular. Though we can't be dogmatic, it makes hermeneutical sense to interpret both instances of "seed" the same way.

In Revelation 12, John wrote about a great sign in heaven depicting a woman who is about to give birth to a baby boy. He also mentioned that a great red dragon was awaiting the birth of the child so he could destroy him. I cover this in more detail in *The Non-Prophet's Guide™ to the Book of Revelation*, but would like to briefly mention it here: Many theologians see the woman, child,

and dragon as symbols representing individuals (Mary, Jesus, Satan) while simultaneously representing corporate entities (Israel, the church, and the end-times world system of the dragon/antichrist).

When we compare Genesis 3:15 with Revelation 12, it seems they are the two bookends of the same prophetic story arc. Revelation 12 (and the end-time events it describes) represents the culmination of this grand narrative found in Scripture. This sheds further light on Genesis 3:15, helping us to see that it, too, could be referring to the "seed" or "offspring" as both individual and corporate entities. In this sense, the Bible is a complete record of spiritual warfare through the ages.

While the philosophy of globalism and talk of elite influencers in the shadows of geopolitics used to be considered the stuff of conspiracy theories, it is now well documented, undeniable, and out in the open for anyone who dares to take a look. A one-world government would logically have a one-world leader. Truly, the groundwork for the end-times figure known as the antichrist has largely been laid.

Technological and Genetic Corruption

In Daniel's interpretation of Nebuchadnezzar's dream about world history as seen through chronological prophetic events related to world empires, a revived Roman Empire of sorts is represented by the feet that are a mixture of iron and clay. This loose conglomeration of nation-states (some strong, some weak) attempting to stay united is what we should see just before the ten toes (most likely ten world regions, countries, or elite rulers) emerge in the aftermath of the rapture.

CLUB OF ROME'S 10 REGIONS

We find a very curious verse in Daniel 2 that is easily overlooked in the context of these ten toes. Speaking specifically of the toes, verse 43 reads, "Just as you saw the iron mixed with baked clay, so the people will be a mixture and will not remain united, any more than iron mixes with clay."

While that rendering from the NIV may not seem all that strange, it begs explanation. If we look at the original Hebrew text to interpret this verse literally, we find that the NASB and KJV render it more accurately. The NASB says "they will combine with one another in the seed of men." The KJV says "they shall mingle themselves with the seed of men."

Based on a literal reading of Daniel 2:43, it appears that in the last days there will be some kind of widespread genetic manipulation going on. If you will recall our earlier studies of Genesis 6, where we read about fallen angels mating with human women, and Genesis 10–11, when Nimrod rebelled against God, built a "gate of the gods," and somehow began to change into a Nephilimic sort of being, it seems this aspect of spiritual warfare could reemerge in the end times.

Prophecy experts and theologians vary widely on what this means, but I mention it because the statement in Daniel 2:43 is in Scripture and therefore it is worthy of our study. Again, we can't ignore parts of Scripture that are tough to study or appear strange to us. Every nuance of every verse is ordained by God and placed in His divine record for a reason.

If the corruption of the human genome was indeed the goal, it seems that each time the enemy has attempted this feat, God has put a stop to the cosmic mischief and closed off that specific avenue of attempted human corruption. The Genesis 6 technology (if you want to call it that) seems to be different than that found in Genesis 11. And Daniel 2:43 appears to indicate another attempt at this during the end times, whereby human DNA is mixed with something foreign that corrupts it yet again. If that is the case, then this future development will fit an age-old spiritual warfare agenda.

Could this be the means by which the antichrist will come back to life after receiving his deadly wound (Zechariah 11:17; Revelation 13:3)? Could it have something to do with the mark of the beast, which cuts people off from the possibility of salvation and later leads to terrible sores on their bodies (Revelation 13:16; 14:9-11; 16:2)? Does it shed light on the statement in Revelation about people wanting to die but not being able to (Revelation 9:4-6)?

Admittedly these questions are speculative in nature, and we can't be dogmatic or build clear theology when we have so little information to work with. But as I mentioned above, these things are worthy of note and healthy to wrestle with. In my opinion, this is not wild or sensational speculation, but a sincere asking of questions about biblical texts we simply can't avoid. Could it be that the significance of these texts is slowly coming to light as we see the stage being set for earth's final era?

In Daniel 12, in a passage about the end times, we read that Daniel was confused by what he saw and heard. We read this powerful and telling exchange as Daniel pondered what was being stated:

> I heard, but I did not understand. So I asked, "My lord, what will the outcome of all this be?" He replied, "Go your way, Daniel, because *the words are rolled up and sealed until the time of the end.* Many will be purified, made spotless and refined, but the wicked will continue to be wicked. None of the wicked will understand, but *those who are wise will understand*" (verses 8-10, emphasis added).

As we draw closer to earth's final moments, it would make sense that certain details previously hidden or misunderstood in Scripture will be progressively unsealed and understood.

SIGN OF THE TIMES

With the discovery of the structure and function of DNA by James Watson and Francis Crick in the 1950s, the possibility of genetic manipulation entered a new era. Currently there are governments openly manipulating and mixing DNA in ways never before possible. The newly available CRISPR-Cas9 technology allows researchers, labs, governments, geneticists, and uncredentialled individuals to edit the genome in specific, targeted, and previously unheard-of ways. At the same time, a movement known as transhumanism—which seeks to use emerging technology, DNA manipulation, and other means to evolve the human race beyond its current physical and mental limitations—is growing rapidly and is being embraced by thought leaders and influencers around the world.

Spiritual Conditions

Scripture speaks of a one-world religion in the end times, and tells us that the antichrist will have a false prophet supporting him. Satan, the antichrist, and the false prophet will make up a counterfeit unholy trinity. The false prophet will be a religious leader who will usher in a global religion—one that accepts all beliefs (except biblical Christianity). This future global religion will absorb the networks and platforms of historic Christianity, but it will be completely apostate. Its oppression of those who don't conform to the globalist agenda will be violent and unbending.

Occult practices will be allowed, encouraged, and celebrated by the coming one-world religion. Demonic worship and activity will proliferate like never before, as will drug use, sexual immorality, murder, theft, greed, and every other cultural vice. Society will continue to devolve into complete moral, spiritual, and relational chaos.

The martyrdom and persecution of Christians and Jews will be the worst it has ever been. The Holocaust of World War 2 is but a snapshot of the murderous conditions Christians and Jews will face during the tribulation.

We are told that after the rapture there will be a great deception that is so pervasive that it is referred to in Scripture simply as "the lie." Second Thessalonians 2:9 says, "The coming of the lawless one will be in accordance with how Satan works. He will use all sorts of displays of power through signs and wonders that serve the lie."

For nearly two centuries, the lie of evolution has slowly and steadily infiltrated the philosophies and belief systems of governments and academia. Various global and religious leaders have pushed for an inclusive acceptance of all belief systems. The occult is on display through many of our music and entertainment icons, and even in the darkened halls of some governments. Christianity in the West is waning while pockets of last-days awakenings are occurring in some of the darkest spiritual strongholds on the planet. Iran, China, and other strongly anti-Christian nations are experiencing explosive underground spiritual revivals. The global persecution of Christians (primarily in Africa, the Mideast, and Asia) has never been worse, and anti-Semitism continues to spread worldwide at a frightening pace.

Prophetic Alignment of Nations

In the end times, all eyes will be on Israel and the Middle East. There will be a satanically inspired hatred for Israel and the Jewish people. This intense spiritual warfare—which has played out for thousands of years—will reach its peak during the tribulation period. By the end of this time, all the nations of earth will be against Israel.

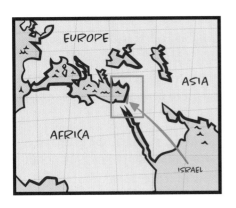

Ezekiel 38–39 details an attack on Israel after its rebirth as a nation (Ezekiel 36–37). This invasion will be led by Russia, Iran, and Turkey and will come from Israel's northern border (from Syria). This will

probably occur soon after the rapture or in the early stages of the tribulation period, although some prophecy experts believe it could happen just prior to, or simultaneous with, the rapture of the church. Israel's enemies will be supernaturally destroyed in this pre-eminent end-times war (Ezekiel 38:18–39:6).

EZEKIEL 38 NATIONS
AND THEIR MODERN-DAY EQUIVALENTS

ANCIENT NAME	MODERN NAME
MAGOG	RUSSIA, CENTRAL ASIA
ROSH	RUSSIA
MESHECH	RUSSIA
TUBAL	RUSSIA OR TURKEY
PERSIA	IRAN
CUSH	ETHIOPIA, SUDAN
LUD	LIBYA, ALGERIA
GOMER	TURKEY
TOGARMAH	TURKEY, CENTRAL ASIA

With the world's attention on Israel, this intense obsession to destroy the nation will increase further and focus on Jerusalem and the Temple Mount. At the midpoint of the tribulation period, the antichrist will enter the holiest part of the rebuilt temple in Jerusalem and defile it in a major way (Daniel 9:27; 2 Thessalonians 2:4). Then he will turn on the Jewish people in an attempt to completely annihilate them.

The unprecedented alignment of the nations involved in the Middle East cannot be overstated. What we currently see in Syria with the alignment of the Ezekiel 38 players and conditions is the clear and undeniable stage-setting for this future end-times attack. The key prophetic regions of the Middle East, Europe, and Asia—as it pertains to end-times spiritual warfare and eschatology—are exactly as the Bible says they would be in the lead-up to the tribulation.

What Now?

For every end-times spiritual warfare condition listed above, we can read today's headlines and witness them forming before our eyes. This sobering fact should not cause us to fear, but to trust God and pay attention to the times in which we live. These facts provide us with key spiritual warfare intel and give some insight into what phase of this cosmic battle we're in. As we witness this unprecedented convergence of end-times spiritual warfare events and conditions, how now should we live? How do we respond to what is taking place? That's what we'll address in the next and final chapter of this book.

CHAPTER 19

Your Personal Marching Orders

"You therefore must endure hardship as a good soldier of Jesus Christ. No one engaged in warfare entangles himself with the affairs of this life, that he may please him who enlisted him as a soldier."

2 TIMOTHY 2:3-4 (NKJV)

About 10 years ago I joined some friends on a four-team mud-run event put on by the Marines in our neighboring state of South Carolina. Proceeds from the event went to support wounded veterans and their families. The event was a fun experience and had a worthy cause. The course was about 5.5 miles long and had 35 obstacles. Many of the obstacles required crawling through mud, swimming through muddy water, lifting muddy people, and climbing up muddy ropes—hence the name. To make the experience even more "fun," Marine drill instructors were stationed at various locations to yell at participants as they attempted the obstacles. Yes, I did this for fun.

My team and I trained for a few months to get ready for the event. We knew it would be difficult—and embarrassing—if we didn't put the work in when nobody was looking so that we would have the necessary stamina and conditioning when it counted most. There is something about having a challenging goal ahead that tends to drive people toward discipline and hard work. When people catch a clear vision of a specific objective, it makes all the difference and tends to fill the motivational tank.

About halfway through the course I sprained may ankle. I didn't tell anyone and kept going because I had trained so hard for the event and I didn't want to let my team down. After another mile or so, my ankle went mostly numb and I could no longer feel the pain. But by the time I got home that day, it had swelled to about double its normal size—so much so that my daughter called it my "baby elephant foot." My ankle was black and blue for a few weeks after.

One of the mottos repeated often at the event was, "Some come to compete. Some come to complete." My team and I definitely came to complete. There was no way our group of middle-aged folk was going to beat a team of young Marines, but I did come to compete in this sense: I embraced the challenge in order to compete against my own will and against the difficult nature of the run. The challenge and struggle were what made the journey meaningful.

By the time we finished the race we were exhausted, covered in layers of stinky backwoods mud, and a couple of us had injuries—but I would not trade the experience for anything. When the journey got tough, we pressed on because we knew what awaited us at the finish line—fresh water, food, clean showers, dry clothes, and the joy of achieving a difficult but worthy goal that we had set out to accomplish.

That race was a microcosm of the Christian life and the warfare we face as we persevere to the end. At times we may fear the obstacles looming before us. We may receive injuries along the way. We may experience exhaustion and feel like giving up. As the journey and the trials go on, our longing for the finish line will likely grow. But completing the race well becomes that much more meaningful because of the obstacles and battles.

The Fight Is Real

I have some good news and some bad news. First the bad news: The fight you and I are in is very real and deadly. Scripture does not pull punches on this at all. Here are some cold, hard facts from 1 Peter 5:8-9: "Be alert and of sober mind. Your enemy the devil prowls around like a roaring lion looking for someone to devour. Resist him, standing firm in the faith, because you know that the family of believers throughout the world is undergoing the same kind of sufferings." The direct import of this passage is that the enemy wants to do his best to destroy you and every other believer on the planet. The threat is real. The scope is global.

There's something sobering about hearing the unadulterated truth when there is bad news. All peripheral issues seem to instantly fade away as our attention is focused on the reality and finality of certain facts we have to face in life. When a doctor has to utter the words, "You have cancer," or when a loved one dies unexpectedly, there's no easy way to state the fact. Nothing can soften the immediate blow. Nothing can stop the news from having to be delivered. Facing reality head-on is what we are called to do. It's what we must do. Aren't you glad you read that?

Okay, now for the good news.

The Victory Is Assured

The good news is that if we are on the right team, our victory is guaranteed. In 1 John 5:4, we read, "Everyone born of God overcomes the world. This is the victory that has overcome the world, even our faith."

Life is not like a YouTube video that allows you to skip ahead so you can see the end. We aren't able to see the eventual outcome of our current reality. But God is outside of time and has provided us with credible accounts of our origins as well as the end of all things. Scripture is like a divine YouTube video that allows us to see the end of history before it happens. If you have read the end of the canonical book we call the Bible, surely you've noticed one very important fact: We win.

Revelation 11:15 proclaims this wonderful statement: "The kingdom of the world has become the kingdom of our Lord and of his Messiah, and he will reign for ever and ever." There are several other similar verses in Revelation, and the point is this: In the end, God wins it all—and we win it with him. If we have trusted Christ as our Savior, our future victory is 100 percent guaranteed. The down payment to prove this will indeed take place is God's track record of fulfilling all past prophecies with 100 percent accuracy. We will not be disappointed.

The Choice Is Yours

The key to fighting our battles is surrender. That's right, we fight by surrendering—not to the enemy, but to the Lord Jesus Christ. Before we can fight in the strength of the Lord, we must walk in the salvation of Christ. We need to submit our will to his and receive him as Savior. This doesn't mean we'll do it perfectly. In fact, we won't. We will stumble in the battle many times. Thankfully our salvation isn't based on our battle performance; rather, it's based on Christ's finished work on the cross.

I don't want to assume that every person who reads this book already knows Christ. In fact, I pray this book gets into the hands of many who don't yet know him. Perhaps that includes you. If so, you can make the great exchange right now. You can trade your sin debt for the positional holiness of Christ. Like a judge who took off his robe to come down and take our place on the sentencing stand, Jesus already took the punishment for our

sins when he died on the cross. Now he offers us a gift. He won't force us to take it, but he holds it out to us as the offer of a lifetime.

If you have never accepted the Lord's gift of salvation, now is the time. I plead with you to ask Jesus to be your Savior. It's not a matter of how good you are; it's a matter of how good he is. He took all your sin on himself at the cross. You can't be good enough. Only he can. He died as your substitute. He took the rap for you—but you must place your faith in him.

> Romans 5:8—God demonstrates his own love for us in this: While we were still sinners, Christ died for us.

One does not become a Christian by following a formula, but I've found that what I'm about to share is an effective way to explain what it means to receive Christ and become a true Christian. People sometimes make salvation complex, but it's so simple a child can understand it. It's as simple as A, B, C.

Admit that you are a sinner. None of us are perfect. We all fall short. Romans 3:23: "All have sinned and fall short of the glory of God." Romans 6:23: "The wages [payment] of sin is death, but the gift of God is eternal life in Christ Jesus our Lord."

Believe that Jesus is God's Son and that he died on the cross with your sins on him. Romans 5:8: "While we were still sinners, Christ died for us."

Confess Jesus as your Lord. This doesn't mean you will never mess up again. Rather, it means you will serve him and learn his ways as you grow spiritually. Romans 10:9: "If you confess with your mouth the Lord Jesus and believe in your heart that God has raised Him from the dead, you will be saved" (NKJV).

Here's a simple prayer you can say to God. These words aren't magic. Again, this is not a formula. But if these words accurately reflect the motives of your heart, then when you lift up this prayer you will become a Christian. You will have placed your faith in Christ and will have had your sins forgiven. You will look forward to an eternity with Jesus in heaven, and you will avoid the terrible time of tribulation that will soon come to the world. Pray this prayer now.

"Lord Jesus, I admit that I am a sinner. I have sinned against you, and sin separates me from you. I thank you that you died on the cross for me. You took my sins upon you and paid my penalty at the cross. I believe you are who you say you are—God in the flesh. I believe you died for my sins. I want to accept your gift of salvation and, at this moment, I ask you to be my Savior. I thank you for this great forgiveness. I now have new life. I now claim you as my Savior and my Lord. In Jesus's name, amen."

If you just prayed that prayer, you are a new creation. The Bible tells us that heaven is celebrating right now because of your decision (Luke 15:10). The Holy Spirit now indwells you and will guide you and keep you. You won't be perfect, but you are forgiven, and the Lord will never leave you. His work in you has just begun. You are an adopted coheir with Christ. You will one day live and reign with him in the millennial kingdom and forever in eternity. Welcome to the family of God!

Assessing Our Armor

Once someone has become a Christian, it's time to put on the full armor of God that we've studied in this book. None of us wears our armor perfectly. Over time, we get better, and it is always a good idea for us to occasionally take stock and make sure we're not doing anything that undermines the effectiveness of our armor.

When my wife and I became engaged, we went through six weeks of premarital counseling. One of the more fascinating assignments our pastor gave each couple was for us to read 1 Corinthians 13—the love chapter—and rank ourselves and each other on each aspect of love that was listed.

> 1 Corinthians 13:4-7—Love is patient, love is kind. It does not envy, it does not boast, it is not proud. It does not dishonor others, it is not self-seeking, it is not easily angered, it keeps no record of wrongs. Love does not delight in evil but rejoices with the truth. It always protects, always trusts, always hopes, always perseveres.

We were amazed that during the exercise, we had each picked the same weakness for ourselves and each other. Our weakest areas of love were different, but we knew each other well enough that we were able to pinpoint the areas that each of us needed to work on. This was very eye-opening—both in terms of how practical God's Word is, and how multifaceted love is.

I believe we can take a similar approach when we assess our battle-readiness. We can look at the armor Paul describes in Ephesians 6 to assess where we need to focus our battle training to become more effective and stay protected as we face the enemy. Look over the list and the brief descriptions below, then use the graphic provided to prayerfully rank your perceived strength or weakness with each piece of armor.

Belt of Truth

Honesty, integrity, and belief in God's truth strengthens our armor.

1 2 3 4 5 6 7 8 9 10

Body Armor of Righteousness

Establishing distance between us and temptation to avoid impurity strengthens our armor.

1 2 3 4 5 6 7 8 9 10

Shoes of the Gospel of Peace

Choosing gospel-based peace in our attitudes and response to stress strengthens our armor.

1 2 3 4 5 6 7 8 9 10

Helmet of Salvation

Guarding our thoughts and submitting them to God strengthens our armor.

1 2 3 4 5 6 7 8 9 10

Sword of the Spirit

Reading, studying, memorizing, and meditating on God's Word strengthens our armor.

1 2 3 4 5 6 7 8 9 10

Shield of Faith

Developing faith in God's promises replaces worry and strengthens our armor.

1 2 3 4 5 6 7 8 9 10

Prayer

Relying on communication with God to align our will with his and present our needs in a spirit of thanksgiving undergirds all of our armor and greatly influences the direction of the battle.

1 2 3 4 5 6 7 8 9 10

It's a good idea to do this assessment from time to time—particularly when you enter a new season of life, or you've allowed a lot of time to lapse since the last time you checked whether you were using your armor effectively. For example, during my teen years and twenties, I realized I needed to work on making better use of my body armor. Now that I'm a couple decades older and in a different season of life characterized by more responsibility and life pressures, I realize that I need to make more effective use of my shoes. That's because I came to realize that the enemy had been slowly and subtly stealing my peace.

As you review whether you're using your armor effectively, you can come up with a battle plan to strengthen the areas in which you are weak. In my case, the battle plan could include memorizing relevant verses of Scripture about God's peace, being more aware and prayerful about maintaining peace within (because what is in us comes out under pressure and affects those around us), sharing my struggle with a few close friends or accountability partners, finding a short Bible study on the topic of peace, and perhaps reading a Christian book about peace by a trusted author.

Our Painful Problem

Though we know that ultimately, victory is assured, we have a dilemma. We're not there yet. I don't know what you are facing right now, and it is often difficult for us to discern which of our trials comes from the world, the flesh, or the devil. But when it comes to living the Christian life, the enemy leverages anything he can to minimize our witness and effectiveness.

We learn from the example of Job that evidently there are times when God may allow the enemy to afflict us. But we need to remember that the devil is on a leash. He can only do what he is permitted to do, and ultimately, God will use all of our experiences for our future blessing and good.

Job 13:15—Though he slay me, yet will I hope in him.

Back when my daughter was two-and-a-half years old, she fell at a park and received an eye full of mulch along with a few cuts on her eyelid. We took her to the emergency room at a nearby hospital to get care for her eye. The doctors needed to put dye in her eye to determine whether her cornea was scratched. My wife and I had to gently hold our little girl down and keep her head still while the doctors went to work.

They held her eye open, shined bright lights into it, and squirted dye directly into her eye. At her age, she did not understand—or care—why this procedure needed to be done. All our daughter knew was that this was a scary ordeal and people she didn't know were sticking tools and chemicals in her eye. Worst of all, the two people she trusted most were holding her down against her will.

She tried everything to get out of this predicament—from kicking, screaming, and crying to calmly looking me in the eyes and saying, "No thank you, Daddy. No thank you," thinking her calm, polite plea would end the ordeal. It almost did. It took everything I had to hold her sweet little curly-haired head still while the doctors did what needed to be done. As you can imagine, parental tears were shed once the treatment was over, and we held, cradled, and comforted our daughter like never before.

As God's children here on earth, we don't have the perspective to understand why he allows evil, trials, pain, or struggles. We don't know why the enemy is permitted to prowl like a lion seeking for people to devour. But God is both a loving heavenly Father and the Great Physician. The pain and confusion we face in life are all part of a much bigger plan—one that we will understand and appreciate fully when we're on the other side of the veil.

Romans 8:18 reminds us that "our present sufferings are not worth comparing with the glory that will be revealed in us." Today we must accept that truth by faith. One day relatively soon, our faith will turn to sight. That is a truth we can cling to as we continue on through life. No other philosophy or religion answers the question of pain. Biblical Christianity does.

We look forward to the day when it all makes sense. In the meantime, we live as strangers in a foreign land—behind enemy lines to help fight the war until our dying breath or until the Lord returns to rapture his bride. We trust even though we don't fully understand. We maintain faith in a God whom we don't see because we see his fingerprints on his creation, history, the Bible, and the changed lives of countless believers.

Will You Advance or Retreat?

As the battle continues to rage, what do you and I plan to do? Will we advance or retreat? Will we huddle together with our shields locked in place and move straight into the battle, or will we play it safe? If we choose to battle, we *will* have targets on our backs, but if we choose the comfort and ease of the sidelines, how can we truly celebrate when the victory is won and the battle is over?

Wouldn't you rather reach the end of the war with some scrapes, bruises, and epic stories of how you persevered? Don't you long to see your commander's face as he says, "Well done, good and faithful servant!

You have been faithful with a few things; I will put you in charge of many things. Come and share your master's happiness!" (Matthew 25:21)?

God uses the battles to stretch us—to make us more like him. Oftentimes our growth appears to be slower than we would like. But if we persevere, we can look back and see how far we've come. This steels our nerves to go the distance.

When it comes to spiritual warfare, the enemy likes to take us by surprise. That is why we need to keep our spiritual armor in a state of readiness. Even so, ultimately, the strength we need for victory comes from God alone. This forces us to rely on his strength and not our own. That way, the Lord gets all the glory, and ultimately, that's what we should desire. We anticipate the day when we can lay our crowns at his feet as an act of total worship. Today we persevere so we'll have such an opportunity.

Note what Paul wrote in 1 Corinthians 9:24-27:

> Don't you realize that in a race everyone runs, but only one person gets the prize? So run to win! All athletes are disciplined in their training. They do it to win a prize that will fade away, but we do it for an eternal prize. So I run with purpose in every step. I am not just shadowboxing. I discipline my body like an athlete, training it to do what it should. Otherwise, I fear that after preaching to others I myself might be disqualified (NLT).

God acknowledges the fact that the battle is tough. He also urges us to have faith in his promises when were in the middle of the explosions, shrapnel, and battlefield smoke. As Paul said in 2 Corinthians 4:8-9, "We are hard pressed on every side, but not crushed; perplexed, but not in despair; persecuted, but not abandoned; struck down, but not destroyed."

God promises not to leave us in the thick of the battle. Philippians 1:6 tells us to be confident "that he who began a good work in you will carry it on to completion until the day of Christ Jesus." And 1 Corinthians 10:13 says, "No temptation has overtaken you except what is common to mankind. And God is faithful; he will not let you be tempted beyond what you can bear. But when you are tempted, he will also provide a way out so that you can endure it."

As believers, the best choice we can make is to trust God and endure the heat of the battle. God promises he will be with us. He will not allow us to face more than we can handle. In the end, he will work all things for our good. And he promises that evil will one day be fully and perfectly dealt with.

As you endure, "be strong in the Lord and in his mighty power" (Ephesians 6:10). Finish strong, my fellow warrior. You'll be glad you did.

What, then, shall we say in response to these things?
If God is for us, who can be against us?…
In all these things we are more than conquerors
through him who loved us.

—Romans 8:31,37

NOTES

Chapter 1—Pre-Genesis History
1. Yogi Berra quotes as cited at https://ftw.usatoday.com/2019/03/the-50-greatest-yogi-berra-quotes.
2. Todd Hampson, *The Non-Prophet's Guide™ to the End Times* (Eugene, OR: Harvest House Publishers, 2018), 21.

Chapter 2—Angels and Fallen Angels Explained
1. Robert Jastrow, *God and the Astronomers* (New York: W.W. Norton, 1978), 116.
2. Nathan Jones, *The Mighty Angels of Revelation* (McKinney, TX: Lamb & Lion Ministries, 2019).

Chapter 4—Genesis 6 and the Pre-Flood World
1. *Ark Encounter*, Answers in Genesis, https://arkencounter.com/flood/myths/.
2. *Strong's Concordance, New American Standard Exhaustive Concordance*, and *Brown-Driver-Briggs Hebrew and English Lexicon*, https://biblehub.com.
3. Michael Belknap and Tim Chaffey, "How Could All the Animals Fit on the Ark?," Answers in Genesis, https://answersingenesis.org/noahs-ark/how-could-all-animals-fit-ark/.

Chapter 5—Babylon Revisited
1. Todd Hampson, *The Non-Prophet's Guide™ to the Book of Revelation* (Eugene, OR: Harvest House Publishers, 2019), 154.
2. Hampson, *The Non-Prophet's Guide™ to the Book of Revelation*, 155-156.
3. Hampson, *The Non-Prophet's Guide™ to the Book of Revelation*, 156.

Chapter 6—Epic Battles in the Unseen Realm
1. "Map of the Least Developed Countries (LDCs)," *United Nations Conference on Trade and Development*, https://unctad.org/en/Pages/ALDC/Least%20Developed%20Countries/LDC-Map.aspx.

Chapter 9—The Believer's Authority over Darkness
1. C.S. Lewis, *Mere Christianity* (New York: Harper Collins, 1952, repr. 2001), 46.

Chapter 10—Ephesians 6
1. James Lloyd, "Roman Army," *Ancient History Encyclopedia*, https://www.ancient.eu/Roman_Army/.
2. "What was life like in the Roman army?," *Bitesize*, https://www.bbc.co.uk/bitesize/articles/zqbnfg8.
3. "Legion," *The Editors of Encyclopedia Britannica*, https://www.britannica.com/topic/legion.

Chapter 11—The Belt of Truth
1. Ron Rhodes, "Manuscript Evidence for the Bible's Reliability," *Reasoning from the Scriptures Ministries*, http://ronrhodes.org/articles/manuscript-evidence-for-the.html.

Chapter 14—The Shield of Faith
1. Graham Land, "3 Kinds of Ancient Roman Shields," *HistoryHit*, https://www.historyhit.com/kinds-of-ancient-roman-shields/.
2. "Timothy Bradley & Teddy Atlas—WE ARE FIREMEN!," *YouTube*, https://www.youtube.com/watch?v=sq2figwIX9s.

Chapter 16—The Sword of the Spirit
1. "Bible Sunday," *Bible Society*, https://www.biblesociety.org.uk/content/get_involved/bible_sunday/2016_resources/Bible-Sunday-Sermon-notes.pdf.

Chapter 17—Prayer
1. "Special Operations Command (SOCOM): Overview," https://www.military.com/special-operations/socom-special-operations-command.html.
2. "Technology of Communication Timeline," Northwest University, https://eagle.northwestu.edu/faculty/gary-gillespie/technology-of-communication-timeline/.
3. "History of Mobile Cell Phones," *BeBusinessed*, https://bebusinessed.com/history/history-cell-phones/.
4. "The History and Evolution of the Smartpone: 1992-1018," *Text Request*, https://www.textrequest.com/blog/history-evolution-smartphone/.
5. Sam Walter Foss, "The Prayer of Cyrus Brown," at https://www.bartleby.com/380/poem/214.html.

Also by Todd Hampson

The Non-Prophet's Guide™ to the End Times

Do you struggle with understanding all the prophecies about the last days? Does it feel like words such as *rapture* and *apocalypse* fly right over your head? You're not alone. It's common to dismiss these and other topics related to Bible prophecy as irrelevant and...well...too complicated.

But *The Non-Prophet's Guide™ to the End Times* changes all that! Prepare to be blessed in an entertaining and meaningful way as this book combines engaging illustrations and down-to-earth explanations to help you navigate the ins and outs of Bible prophecy. There's no better time to grasp God's plan the future—and for you—than this very moment.

The Non-Prophet's Guide™ to the End Times Workbook

If you're ready to dig deeper into what the Bible has to say about the end times and gain insight into what God has planned for the future, let *The Non-Prophet's Guide™ to the End Times Workbook* be your guide.

With this resource, you'll have the opportunity to unpack the many questions people ask about the last days, such as...

- How does fulfilled Bible prophecy affect our view of yet-to-be-fulfilled Bible prophecy?
- What can we learn from those who were eyewitnesses of Jesus's first coming?
- How can we know whether today's events were mentioned in Bible prophecy?
- How can we discern the difference between conspiracy theories and facts when we attempt to determine the signs of the end times?

A great way to increase your knowledge of all God has planned for the future!

The Non-Prophet's Guide™ to the Book of Revelation

If the final book of the Bible has ever left you scratching your head or wondering what to make of plagues and horsemen, your friendly Non-Prophet is here to help you read Revelation as never before.

Full of fascinating content and graphics, you'll find this a user-friendly guide to the apostle John's prophecies about the last days. This concise and appealing study...

- removes the fear factor and demystifies the capstone book of the Bible
- provides biblical clarity about the key events in the end times
- helps reclaim your hope, confidence, and joy in the promised future

The last days are nearer than ever before. There's no better time to understand the present in light of history's final outcome.